Praise for

Inspiring, illuminating, and uplifting, Alan Cohen brings sheer joy to the topic of spiritual communication! Whether you're interested in angels, passed over loved ones, spirit guides, or the Divine itself, Alan's years of experience and natural wisdom go straight to the heart in a way that is practical and easy to understand. Friends in High Places *erases the fear, doubt, and confusion that many experience when developing their spiritual gifts. Alan's thoughtful and kind way of explaining concepts like channeling, mediumship, intuitive guidance, and psychic connections will save you lots of time and struggle and send you joyfully on your way to success and a deeply enriched spiritual path. Trust me, this book is pure magic!*

—Radleigh Valentine, Bestselling author
and spiritual teacher

I love this book. I've almost finished it in one sitting! I know it will be immensely helpful to so many people. Each one of us has wise and loving guidance available to us whenever we need it. Friends in High Places *gently moves aside the veil to show us the many ways we can access this wisdom. It's filled with hope, prayers, down-to-earth examples and many techniques. Your friends in high places want to help. This book shows you how to listen.*

—Lynn A. Robinson, author of *Divine Intuition:
Your Inner Guide to Purpose, Peace and Prosperity*

Alan Cohen is a brilliant storyteller. Friends in High Places *illustrates the help available to all of humanity about how to navigate the multisensory world. He naturally leads readers through a series of exercises to gently remind you of the incredible encounters available to you in the spirit world. You will love this book!*

—Marie Manuchehri, RN, author of *Intuitive Self-Healing*
and *How to Communicate with Your Spirit Guides*

Friends In High Places *had me totally intrigued. I could not put it down. Alan Cohen's fascinating recollections of his encounters with the other side is written so fluently and vividly, I felt like I was there. His perception and explanations of his celestial experiences is not only thought provoking, but he also magically weaves his words for the reader to make sense of it all in a grounded and helpful way. Absolutely brilliant!'*

—Liz Winter, professional medium and author of
Keeping Love Alive on the Other Side

Friends In High Places *is a soulful, practical look into the world of channeling and spirituality. Alan empowers the reader by demonstrating how to spot true divine wisdom. He kindly shares his personal adventures with fascinating teachers while gently guiding the reader to remember that the purest information comes from within.*

— Dougall Fraser, award-winning intuitive
and author of *Your Life In Color*

A phenomenal book! A very deep and personal account that speaks directly to me. The Bible instructs us to "test the spirits." Bravo to Alan Cohen for stepping up and reminding us of the value—and the need for discernment—regarding interdimensional communication.

—Christopher Naughton, Emmy® award-winning producer
and author of *America's Next Great Awakening:
A New American Revolution in Consciousness*

Also by Alan Cohen

Are You as Happy as Your Dog?
A Course in Miracles Made Easy
Dare to Be Yourself
A Deep Breath of Life
A Daily Dose of Sanity
Don't Get Lucky, Get Smart
The Dragon Doesn't Live Here Anymore
Enough Already
The Grace Factor
Handle with Prayer
Happily Even After
Have You Hugged a Monster Today?
I Had It All the Time
How Good Can It Get?
Joy Is My Compass
Lifestyles of the Rich in Spirit
Linden's Last Life
Looking in for Number One
The Master Keys of Healing
My Father's Voice
The Peace That You Seek
Relax into Wealth
Rising in Love
Setting the Seen
Soul and Destiny
Spirit Means Business
The Tao Made Easy
Why Your Life Sucks and What You Can Do about It
Wisdom of the Heart

FRIENDS
IN
HIGH PLACES

A BREAKTHROUGH GUIDE TO
INTERDIMENSIONAL COMMUNICATION

FRIENDS
IN
HIGH PLACES

A Breakthrough Guide to Interdimensional Communication

ALAN COHEN

Published in the United States by Alan Cohen Publications
www.alancohen.com

Cover design: Elena Karampouli • Interior design: Riann Bender

ISBN 978-0-910367-10-3

E-book ISBN: 978-0-910367-12-7

Printed in the United States of America

To all the spiritual masters, visible and invisible, who guide humanity, relieve suffering, and hold the torch of truth to bring the world closer to heaven

CONTENTS

INTRODUCTION

When I ask my seminar audiences, "Who among you has experienced some kind of communication or guidance from a dimension beyond the material world?" nearly everyone in the audience raises their hand. Perhaps so would you. You think about a friend you have not seen in a long time, and minutes later you get a phone call or email from that person. Or you have received some uncanny sign that a loved one who has passed on is still very much with you. When you write, paint, or play music, you sense that some higher power is moving through you rather than you originating the work. Maybe you have gone through a devastating breakup, the loss of a dear friend, a health issue, unexpected job ending, or financial setback that has motivated you to ask deeper questions about your life. You may be disappointed or disgusted with a world filled with fear, disease, and war, and you cannot believe this is the way God meant for us to live. You might even demand that the universe show you what stands behind the curtain of illusion that shields most people from the truth.

Perhaps you are already well-established on your spiritual path. Invisible dimensions are real to you, and you want to navigate them more skillfully. You may feel confused or overwhelmed with the smorgasbord of information, guidance, and predictions laid before you. Which teachers are true, and which are fake? Which prophecies can you trust? Was that really your departed mother speaking to you in that psychic reading? How can you apply higher wisdom to your daily activities, live true to your unique path, and avoid detours, delays, and supernatural snares?

You might have already stepped into the role of teacher, reader, psychic, channeler, or healer, and you want to deliver the richest gifts to your audience. You want to be sure that your guidance is correct, walk your talk, and let the words you speak drop into your heart and your experience. You want to banish doubt and master your craft. You may wish that someone would help you as much as you are helping your clients or students.

The book you are holding will provide you with a roadmap to navigate worlds beyond the obvious. I will answer many of your questions and help you make the supernatural natural, the paranormal normal, and the extrasensory sensory. You are not crazy, after all. What you thought was wrong with you may be what's right with you. If you don't fit in with the mainstream, you belong to a greater stream. If you believe there has to be more to life than the one you've been shown, you are more in touch with reality than most people who settle for the world they've been given rather than one they choose. There are many, many people—far more than you know—whose life extends beyond the material plane. Consider this book a deep validation of you, your gut knowing, and your nontraditional choices. You are on track with your purpose.

In the chapters that follow, I will introduce you to six master spiritual teachers who have most profoundly influenced my life. One thing they have in common is that they don't have bodies. They are nonphysical beings who speak through people who serve as channels for the wisdom they impart. Yet the spiritual entities and their channelers are not the object of this writing. The teachings they deliver are far more important than the personages. If you become enamored with the messenger, you might miss the message. We seek truth, not people.

I will intimately describe my relationship with the entities and the channelers, and lay out the life-changing lessons I have learned, so you can apply them to your own journey. I will reveal my successful choices and my mistakes, so you can replicate what works and avoid the traps. While I have enjoyed many advances, I have also been duped by fakes, received false prophecies, given my power away, and seen talented teachers fall. I have learned from all of my teachers, the good, bad, and mediocre. I want you to benefit from my experience, so you can stand on my shoulders and hasten to fulfill your own destiny.

Most important, I want to help you directly connect with authentic spiritual guidance. You have your own unique relationship with mentors, spirit guides, angels, and God. You have more friends in high places than you know. My encounters with nonphysical entities and interdimensional communication are not special and I do not have any undue talents or dispensation. Grace has guided me as it has guided you. The same Higher Power that has connected me with transformational guides has provided for you, and will continue. When all teachers have come and gone, you will be established in your divine self, the exalted soul that you are.

We are about to accelerate your spiritual evolution. Applying the ideas in this book will collapse the amount of time you wander in psychic thickets, and keep you true to your heart's intention. You are about to partner with souls you cannot see, but who know you better than you know yourself—and love you more than you can imagine.

The world of supernatural guidance is not random, and it need not be confusing or overwhelming. It is definitely not spooky. (Truth be told, the physical world in which we have become immersed is far scarier.) The spiritual dimension can be easily mapped, understood, and navigated with the right guidance and sincere intention. Let's pierce beyond the gravitational field of earth into a far more satisfying expanse. If, like me, you have wondered if there is more, you are about to receive a definitive answer. You are ready.

Alan Cohen

PART I

THE QUEST FOR SOMETHING MORE

WISDOM FROM BEYOND THE VEIL

Even as a child I suspected there was life beyond the world I could touch. I remember telling a buddy, "Maybe we are all dead and we are just dreaming we are alive." Now, so many years later, I have come to recognize the truth I uttered, with a crucial variation: We are all fully alive as spiritual beings, dreaming we are but bodies walking through a limited world.

At age fourteen I was living in a horrid neighborhood, associating with friends immersed in foul deeds. I felt alone, empty, and lost. Then I met a young rabbi who enjoyed a genuinely loving relationship with God. He inspired me to become an Orthodox Jew, which gave me a connection to a richer universe than the hollow world I knew. Although I later let go of my religious practices, that period provided my first entrée into a world that transcended the obvious.

As a high school senior, I encountered an amateur hypnotist who took me through a short hypnotic induction. During that process, I relaxed into an extremely peaceful, soul-soothing state of mind. I touched into what I now know to be an alpha brainwave state. My brief taste of profound inner peace intensified my yearning to find a way to capture that feeling again.

In college I was a psychology major, hoping to learn what made me and humanity tick. The subject matter of my courses was boring, insipid, and irrelevant to my life—mostly about rats, statistics, and crazy people. I was learning erudite theories and trendy jargon, but I remained hungry to understand who I am and why I am here. Most of my professors were not happy people. One drove a red Corvette convertible so he could pick up sexy students; several were having affairs with each other; another had a nervous habit that made his eyes wiggle when he spoke; another was a Sigmund Freud clone with a cigar constantly hanging from his lips; another bragged about his Ivy League degree. It seemed to me that most of them could use a good psychologist. I couldn't relate to any of them.

Stage 1 of Spiritual Evolution

You feel lost, alone, and confused. The world seems unfair and overwhelming, you struggle and suffer, and you see no way out of a hellish existence. You assume a victim position, feeling trapped and manipulated by external forces greater than yourself. You flounder with the masses, and can't imagine escaping from the painful situations in which you find yourself enmeshed.

Amidst my lackluster classes, I was determined to keep myself stimulated. I signed up for a senior course that allowed me to do an independent research project. I had been reading a fascinating book, *The Search for Bridey Murphy,* the true story of an Irish woman who recalled her previous lives, substantiated by significant documentation. I set up an experiment in which I guided subjects on a hypnotic age regression. While the psychology piece sought to examine how the subjects replicated childhood handwriting and picture-drawing, I added the supernatural element of regressing them to past lives. To my delight, the subjects came up with all kinds of fascinating previous incarnations.

I took a yoga class that concluded with a long guided deep relaxation. For those minutes my mind, usually racing in five directions at once, became still. I touched into the same blissful state I discovered when I was hypnotized. The taste of heaven was becoming more familiar to me, and I was gaining confidence that I could access it at will.

During that time, I had a dream that my father was going to die in five weeks. Five weeks later, to the day, he died suddenly. While I was saddened by my father's passing, I gained confirmation that there are ways of knowing things, including future events, that the intellect cannot access. And if there are realms beyond the physical senses—"In my Father's house there are many mansions"—then my dad remained alive at another frequency, and I could communicate with him, which I did.

Driven to widen my path of enlightenment, I found my way to a humanistic psychology program in graduate school. This coursework, a night-and-day contrast with my undergraduate studies, was founded on relating to people, not rats, and stretching to fulfill our highest potential. The professors were authentic people who cared about students and recognized the value of self-expression, communication, and following a passionate path. After sixteen years of education that had stuffed my head with irrelevant facts but left my soul out in the cold, I felt like I had finally come home.

A fellow student introduced me to Ram Dass, a revered spiritual teacher who had once been a neurotic Jewish psychologist— I could relate—but dropped out and found his way to a guru in India who utterly changed his life. As I studied before-and-after photos in Ram Dass's classic book *Be Here Now*, I observed a man who had been reborn as a being of effulgent light. Ram Dass's guru, Neem Karoli Baba, affectionately known as Maharaj-ji, knew everything in Ram Dass's mind, and loved him unconditionally. At one time, for example, Ram Dass was traveling on a bus in India with a group of 23 of his students plus the driver, when they unexpectedly encountered Maharaj-ji at a festival. Maharaj-ji guided the group to a home where he was staying, where that morning he had instructed the householder to prepare 25 additional places for dinner—all orchestrated before the bus had arrived.

Titillated by Maharaj-ji's psychic powers, I dove into studentship with Ram Dass. But eventually I discovered that the psychic element was just the bait to get me into the schoolroom of soul awakening. As I practiced yoga, meditation, prayer, and healing, my heart opened to a life of joy and integrity. After a while, psychic powers seemed more like introductory material. A spirit-based life was the real treasure.

When I learned that Hilda Charlton, a woman in New York City, was a companion teacher to Ram Dass, I attended one of her classes. This led to an intensive fourteen-year study with this spiritual master. Hilda enjoyed relationships with a coterie of invisible angels, saints, entities, and ascended masters far more real to her than physical bodies. This extraordinary teacher served as a bridge to the etheric world for me and thousands of others who sensed that reality spanned far beyond frightful newscasts. The more I studied with Hilda, the thinner became the veil between the worlds.

Then I was contacted by Carla Gordan, a gifted trance medium. While I had had a few readings by relatively untalented psychics, Carla's channeling proved to me beyond a shadow of a doubt that there are benign, compassionate spiritual entities who can short-cut our suffering and advance our spiritual growth at light speed. My eighteen-year study with Carla and her guides gave me a wealth of information to navigate my spiritual journey, but even more important, self-trust and faith in God that has proven to be the foundation of my life.

Around the time I met Carla, *A Course in Miracles* came into my life. While I was initially skeptical about this document, as I started to study it I realized that it came from a source far beyond the world. The author identified himself as Jesus Christ, speaking to humanity to underscore the healing power of forgiveness and correct misperceptions about who he is and what he wants people to know about how to live. That book was channeled by a professor of medical psychology who was a self-described Jewish atheist skeptic. Yet she had an agreement with Jesus at the soul level to deliver this immensely important teaching to the world.

All of these encounters have led me to several important conclusions that I would like to solidify for you in this book:

1. The nonphysical or spiritual dimension is absolutely real, in many ways more substantial than the three-dimensional world we regard as so solid.

2. There exist beings, entities, and streams of consciousness who are willing, able, and eager to assist you on your spiritual journey even while you walk through the material world.

3. Interdimensional conversations require strong intention and discernment to maximize results and avoid detours and pitfalls.

4. The Higher Power that speaks through intermediaries also speaks to you directly. You can access divine guidance from within your own mind and heart.

Now let's meet the guides and their channels, but most important, let's make the wisdom and love they reveal our own.

PART II

CARLA AND THE GUIDES:

YOU DO NOT WALK ALONE

CONTACT AND CONFIRMATION

"Go to the Jamison Mortuary and tell the undertaker Mr. Williams that we've received his letter," the invisible spirit spoke clearly. "Tell him the answer to his question is 'Yes.'"

Carla and Helen looked at each other, stunned. They had never heard of the Jamison Mortuary, they did not know Mr. Williams, and they had no idea what his question was. They had simply beseeched the guide, "Can you please give us some sign that what we are doing is authentic, and will somehow help people?"

Dr. Carla Gordan was a psychologist and minister who prayed daily with her associate Helen Thomas Irwin. One day during their prayer session, Carla saw a burst of white light descending toward her head. The light morphed into the form of a dove and pierced her forehead like a flash of lightning. Then she blanked out and lost all awareness of what was happening in the room around her.

When Carla finally regained consciousness, she saw Helen sitting before her, her face wet with tears, a pile of used tissues in her lap. "Are you alright?" Carla asked, shocked and concerned.

Helen shot her a stunned look. "You mean you don't know what just happened?"

Carla shook her head.

"For the last three hours you've given me the most important information anyone has ever told me about my life. You accessed the most intimate details I've never told anyone. You answered my deepest questions and left nothing untouched."

Carla was speechless. All she had experienced was the dove entering her forehead. What was going on here?

Now I Can Die in Peace

Astounded by their weird but intriguing experience, Carla and Helen attempted to replicate the spontaneous channeling session. With some practice, Carla found that she could say a prayer and consciously induce her trance. The two women continued the sessions, each encounter yielding more information—and raising more questions. *How am I getting information I could not possibly know? Who or what is the source of this information? Is the source real and benevolent, or have I broken something in my brain?*

The two women decided to test the entity's message. One night Carla and Helen nervously made their way to the Jamison Mortuary, with no idea who or what they would find. Carla forced herself to knock on the mortuary door. Soon a man answered. When he introduced himself as the undertaker Mr. Williams, the women stiffened.

The ladies invited themselves in and told the mortician their outlandish story, wondering if they were crazy or misguided. Carla concluded with the message from the guide: "We've received your letter. The answer to your question is 'Yes.'"

Mortician Roy Williams blanched. The women waited anxiously as he rose and walked to the small refrigerator in his office, poured himself a shot of whisky, and tried to gather himself. He told the ladies, "Very few people know this, but I am dying. I have been wondering constantly about what will happen to me after I die. One day before a funeral I wrote a letter to God, asking, 'Is there life after death?' I sealed the letter and placed it in the jacket pocket of the deceased in the coffin, which was soon buried. No one ever saw the letter and I told no one about it."

The two women, like you right about now, were covered with goosebumps.

"Thank you so much for your message," Roy Williams told the ladies, tears in his eyes. "God has answered my question through you. Now I can die in peace."

How can a human being know more than what the physical senses reveal? What vast intelligent source can reach into a person's soul and deliver guidance to relieve pain and make lives better? Who was speaking through Carla Gordan and others like her? Can you, too, tap into a source of wisdom and love from beyond the earth, use it to create healing for yourself, and deliver blessings to others? Let us now part the curtain between dimensions and clear the way for you to receive answers to the most important questions of your life.

We are about to step into our first Direct Connect *exercise. Each chapter will include at least one introspective practice session to help you apply the principles of the chapter to your life. The goal of all the* Direct Connect *experiences is to strengthen your ability to access your own guidance and claim the path your innate wisdom reveals.*

DIRECT CONNECT 1
Recognizing, Trusting, and Acting on Guidance

Have you ever received guidance from a source beyond your normal thinking mind?

How did that message come to you?

What did that source tell you?

Who or what do you believe was the source of that guidance?

Did you act on that guidance? If so, what happened? If you did not act on it, what happened?

What do you feel you are being guided to do in your life now?

What would be your next step to follow that guidance?

✦ ✦ ✦

Speak this affirmation or one like it in your own words:

*I open to receive accurate, helpful guidance
from a benevolent source
beyond my intellect and physical senses.*

*I put aside anxious effort, relax, and allow my deeper self to
show me what I need to know.*

I trust that I am loved and I am guided.

INTERDIMENSIONAL COMMUNICATION

Without planning it, Carla Gordan had spontaneously stepped into the role of a *full-trance medium*. When she went into her altered state of consciousness, she experienced a restful dream state, during which she would visit a pleasant scene like a library or a park. Meanwhile she was completely unaware of the information she voiced, and she remembered not a word of it afterward. She awoke feeling alert and refreshed. Over the thirty-five-year period that followed, Carla gave thousands of readings while in trance, with uncanny accuracy, bringing inspiration, healing, and hope to her clients.

Mediumship and channeling run through recorded history and surely go back farther. The Old and New Testaments are filled with prophets and prophecies, as are the sacred books of all religions, most of which were established by an individual who received messages from beyond Earth. Moses received the Ten Commandments directly from God on Mount Sinai. The Prophet Mohammed was given the Qur'an by the Angel Gabriel. The Oracle at Delphi was considered the definitive source of divine guidance during her epoch; the highest-ranking leaders consulted her before making any important decisions. Jesus prophesied his crucifixion and resurrection. Even today His Holiness the Dalai Lama, one of the great spiritual leaders of our time, consults a trance-induced medium at the beginning of each year.

We know spirit-guided teachers by many different names: channelers, mediums, seers, spiritualists, clairvoyants, intuitives, telepaths, mystics, and psychics. Yet the dynamics behind all such phenomena are similar: A human being taps into a source of higher wisdom and delivers valuable information to those in need of help and healing.

Partial Trance Mediums

Some mediums attain a partial trance rather than a full one. During their channeling they remain somewhat conscious and hear the words being spoken. Some mediums feel fully present and are clearly aware of the transmission, as if they are sitting in a room listening to a lecture. Others hear the words more vaguely, as if at a distance. While full-trance mediums remember nothing of what was said, partial trance mediums may remember some or all of what was said.

Tuning to Your Own Channel

It is tempting to bow at the feet of channelers and worship them as if they have a unique dispensation from God. In a way they do, in that they have a gift that can benefit many people, and they deserve profound appreciation and respect for their talents and services.

At the same time, we must recognize the capacity we all have to receive guidance from higher realms. In a sense, everyone channels. You may not go into trance and give voice to an invisible entity, but you do receive guidance that proceeds from a source beyond your thinking mind. You get inklings, urges, intuitions, hunches, and inclinations. When you hear a certain teaching or word of advice, you may get goosebumps. You may experience a dream, flash, or vision. You may sense that a loved one who has passed on is sending you a message. You may have precognition of an event that later occurs just as you saw it in your mind's eye beforehand. At key moments in your life, the veil between worlds parts and a ray of wisdom shines through that brings you guidance and encouragement.

The Courage to Come Forth

A high school teacher used to invite me to her classes to talk about the paranormal. During the class, I would ask students if any of them had any psychic experiences, precognitions, or encounters with nonphysical entities. No one raised their hand. Then after class a line of students would form to tell me of their psychic experiences. "After my grandma died, I heard her whisper in my ear while I was falling asleep." "When I hear my phone ring, I can tell who is calling before I look at caller ID." "I know that certain things are going to happen, and then they do."

I would ask the students, "Why didn't you share that in class when I asked?" Without fail, the students would answer, "I didn't want the other kids to think I was weird." Meanwhile there was a long line of "weird" kids waiting to talk about their meaningful experiences.

This phenomenon illustrates the double standard in our culture: We are all connected to unseen powers, but only a small percentage of people are willing to publicly acknowledge it. When the U.S. Navy released a video of aircraft carrier U.S.S. Nimitz pilots' encounter with a UFO, all of the major television networks presented a story about it. After the report, every single reporter made some silly joke about aliens. None of them could hold the story, though rife with undeniable facts and vast import, as serious. They all had to siphon off the tension by making fun of the story and invalidating it. Meanwhile that story was viewed online by more readers of the *New York Times* than any other article ever posted in the history of the newspaper's website. Obviously there were many—very many—people who took the encounter quite seriously.

It is time for our culture to break the stigma that clouds authentic paranormal phenomena. We are living at the auspicious moment when our consciousness is expanding to embrace a far larger universe than we once believed we lived in. Many people resist, deny, or seek to discredit psychic phenomena. While some such phenomena are hoaxes worth debunking, a large number are valid and deserve respect. When we welcome friends in high places, they can help us in ways we cannot help ourselves.

DIRECT CONNECT 2

Out of the Spiritual Closet

Do you have a spiritual life, paranormal experiences, or uncommon beliefs you feel shy to reveal to the world?

In what ways do you fear that people would criticize or judge you, make fun of you, or hurt you?

What would you be saying or doing differently if you had more confidence to express your beliefs and follow your guidance?

✦ ✦ ✦

Practice this affirmation or one like it that you create:

I now claim the courage and confidence to walk the spiritual path of my choosing.

I trust the God within me to guide, protect, and prosper me.

I will live the life I choose.

How Do You Receive Guidance?

We all receive guidance, each in our own unique way, with our own personal signs. Some people report that they get a warm rush of energy; or goosebumps; or the hairs on their neck or arms stand up; or they feel a tingling in the back of their head; or a sense of peace fills their heart; or they get so excited about an idea that they must immediately act on it. Others report seeing a tiny blue flash of light. Some hear a whisper. Others get a deep knowing, a good or bad feeling when considering a direction they might take. Regardless of how you receive guidance, the important thing is to recognize that you have access to higher wisdom. When you let yourself receive and act on it, good things happen. Some people receive guidance as compelling inspiration. When you feel moved to play music, write, dance, paint, invent, teach, connect with a particular person, take a significant business step, or purchase a particular item, you may sense that a deeper source is inspiring you. A light bulb flashes over your head and you are off and running with exciting ideas and energy that lead to success. You are channeling.

Creative people acknowledge that their best ideas come from a fountain beyond the world. The word "music" derives from the word "muse," a spiritual guide that stimulates creative acts. The genius Mozart, who composed his first opera at the age of six, later declared, *"It is when I am, as it were, completely myself, entirely alone, and of good cheer . . . that ideas flow best and most abundantly. Whence and how they come, I know not, nor can I force them."* Truly creative people do not claim, "I thought this up all by myself." They admit that their success is a co-creation of their worldly skill and inspiration from a transcendent voice.

Even some very conservative people who would not be considered spiritual or delve into mystical pursuits, acknowledge guidance. When U.S. Army General Colin Powell was asked to run for President of the United States, he declined, citing, "What wasn't pulling me was my inner compass and my sense of who I am." Like General Powell, you and I have an inner compass that points us where we need to go. We just need the courage to act on it.

There is nothing spooky or mysterious about channeling. When you channel with pure intent, no one is possessing you against your will, or enacting a zombie takeover. Authentic channeling is the natural co-creative process between a human personality and the intelligence of the universe. It is the meeting point of person and God, the intersection of spirit and matter via the medium of mind. The famous Michelangelo painting on the ceiling of the Sistine Chapel depicts the finger of God touching the finger of a man. This image symbolizes divine intelligence transmitting truth, beauty, and love to each of us, so we may deliver it to earth. How blessed are we to participate in such a process!

I don't recommend you go poking around the ethers looking for some entity to channel. If you do, you will most likely contact a fantasy, imposter, or compromised spook. (We will explore detours from purposeful channeling in a later chapter.) The best channels I know were simply going about their life, following their spiritual path, when their entity contacted them. If you live with a pure heart and good intent, you will receive inspiration in the way that can most benefit you and others.

When Carla Gordan realized that whoever was speaking through her was trying to make the world a better place, she dedicated her life to delivering her gift to as many people as possible. I was one of them. Now let's find out how you are, as well.

DIRECT CONNECT 3
How Do You Receive Guidance?

Check the boxes that match the ways you know that what you are thinking, hearing, or feeling is important for you to know and act on.

☐ I get goosebumps.

☐ The hairs on my arms or the back of my neck stand up.

☐ I feel a rush of warmth through my heart or body.

☐ I hear a voice or whisper.

☐ I see an image in my mind's eye.

☐ I feel inspired, excited, or passionate when considering a particular action or project.

☐ I see a small blue flash or other color light.

☐ I feel a compelling urge to take a particular action or avoid it.

☐ I am filled with a sense of peace or relief.

☐ I feel as if I am trying on a garment that fits me perfectly.

☐ I get a premonition.

☐ I hear a phrase from a person or read a passage that speaks to me and excites me.

☐ Other: _____

You are more connected to higher wisdom than you realize. You have been receiving guidance your entire life, although you may not have been aware of it. You now stand at a milestone point in your life when you are ready to take Spirit's hand and walk a wider path of confidence, vision, and infinite possibilities. You do not walk alone.

THE SPIRIT WHO SAW INTO MY SOUL

I stood outside the door of Carla Gordan's room, trying to quell my fear of speaking to a spook. I had read and heard about people who talk to the dead, and busted ghosts; now I was about to meet one. Would I be hypnotized or brainwashed? Would some demon jump out of the channeler and take me over, like *The Invasion of the Body Snatchers*? Would I have to call an exorcist? All of the horror movies I watched as a child marched before me like a dime-store Halloween parade. What had I gotten myself into?

Yet Carla had seemed kind and gentle enough when I met her a day earlier at Elizabethtown College in rural Pennsylvania. She felt more like the mom next door than the Wicked Witch of the West. Fiftyish, with a round face complimented by lightly permed medium length brown hair, she wore a stylish blue muumuu and wraparound sunglasses that protected her unusually sensitive eyes. Her speech revealed a slight southern twang, punctuated by irreverent laughter and a blend of caring and sass. I liked her.

Carla had read my book *The Dragon Doesn't Live Here Anymore*, and sent me a letter telling me she would like to meet me and give me a reading. When we found that we would both be teaching at the Spiritual Frontiers Fellowship conference, we decided to connect. Little did I realize what a date with destiny that meeting would prove to be.

I gathered myself, took a deep breath, and knocked on Carla's dormitory door. When she answered, my solar plexus started to unclench. She was down home and easy to be with, free of pretense. She smiled and ushered me to an empty chair beside a cheap student desk fastened to a green pastel cinder block wall. After a few moments of pleasantries, Carla took a seat facing me and pinned a lavalier microphone to her blouse. She reached for a cassette recorder on the table beside her and pressed Record. The woman closed her eyes and said a prayer that would become oh so familiar and comforting to me in the many years that followed:

Let's relax together and feel the presence
of a living, loving God.
In this moment of time, we ask to lift beyond earth
into areas of absolute truth.
I ask that the things most needed by this soul
in this time will be spoken.
I ask to be a channel of love and of blessing.
Thank you, Father.
We stand believing.

A rush of energy coursed through Carla's body as she sat up straighter. Her guide, George, was readying to speak through her. (She later complained that none of her guides had exotic spiritual names. She was stuck with George. The guides later explained that this simple name was intentional, to keep Carla and Helen comfortable with familiar names, since they were already nervous about what they were doing. The guides also did not want Carla or Helen to be enamored or distracted by an exotic spiritual name.)

Soon George began to speak through Carla in a digni-fied quasi-British accent, a far cry from her usual speech. He began to tell me about my life's purpose, past lives, health, and patterns of thought and feeling. At first I was more curi-ous than receptive, trying to discern whether George was for real and if what he had to say was worth hearing. As George went on, I realized that he could see into my soul. He knew me better than I knew myself. I felt no judg-ment nor condemnation—only a stern but compassionate clarity and a sincere desire to help. His insights rang true, and I began to trust his guidance. After a while I forgot that I was communicating with an invisible spirit; I was thrilled to have access to a brilliant mind. Whether or not he had a body was less important than that he had the truth.

Time-Collapse Therapy

I got up the nerve to ask George about the issue most troubling me: an unresolved romantic relationship. A year earlier I had fallen in love with a woman named Dana. While the relationship was initially exciting and heady, it turned into a roller coaster of ecstasy and torment. Dana had gotten divorced during the year before we met and she was still emotionally wounded, reluctant to fully open herself to another man. I had my own issues. Before I met Dana, I had been a celibate yogi, and entering an intimate relation-ship was a huge vulnerable shift for me. I was immature in relationships. Dana and I would get together for romantic dates and then retreat to our separate corners for long peri-ods of time. Neither of our communication skills were good, so the relationship took a long, excruciating on-again-off-again course. For an entire year I was in heaven for brief moments and in hell for long interludes. Dana felt the same way. Finally we agreed to part. I told George nothing about this, but simply asked, "How can I come to peace about the relationship I have been in?"

George answered, "Both of you brought fears and hypersensitivity to the relationship. You also matched each other with ambivalence. You both wanted to open your hearts, but it is difficult to establish a healthy relationship where there is so much self-protection. But you were good for each other. Your excitement about being together drew both of you out of the shells you were in. It was a transitional relationship. Be grateful for it, let it go, and move on."

The moment I heard George's explanation, I understood the dynamics behind the relationship that had caused me so much pain. Seeing from a higher perspective, I became free. Immediately I felt healed and complete with the relationship—a huge relief after a year of torment.

Soon the thirty-minute reading was over. (Carla never looked at a clock during her readings but always ended exactly on time.) Her face changed dramatically; the guide had departed like a bird soaring into the sky from a high branch of a tree. Carla got her bearings, shut off the cassette player, and handed me the tape.

"Thank you so much for the very helpful information about my relationship!" I told her.

Carla smiled innocently. "I'm so glad the reading was helpful for you."

The unknowing look on Carla's face tipped me off. "You don't remember what you said, do you?"

"Not a word."

"Where were you?"

Carla laughed. "They take me to a garden or a library. It's quite pleasant."

I stood and walked out of the dorm room, my precious cassette tucked safely in my pocket. In the months that followed I listened to it again and again, understanding more of the information each time. I was amazed at how much the guide had said that went over my head during the reading, but sank in when I later paid more attention to it. Whoever George was, he had saved me from a great deal of confusion and pain. I considered the session equivalent to a year or more of therapy, what it might have taken to slowly peel away layers of fear, density, and ego to get to the core issues of my relationship. I quit wondering whether George was a spook, or some aspect of Carla's mind, or some projection of my own mind—maybe all of the above. He knew what he was talking about, and that was all that mattered. Whatever this was, or wherever it was coming from, it was spiritual gold. I wanted more.

Stage 2 of Spiritual Evolution

You recognize glimmers of a way out of pain. You discover a book, seminar, teacher, or friend that introduces you to higher principles that explain life in ways your previous training failed to illuminate. You gain hope, start to practice newfound principles, and begin to enjoy positive results of your upgraded vision. You sense that your life can become more serene, and you can find greater purpose and meaning.

DIRECT CONNECT 4
Time-Collapse Therapy

Have you struggled for a long time with an issue, situation, or addiction you cannot master by yourself, and traditional approaches or therapies have not helped you to resolve?

If so, what is the issue?

How would your life be better if you could get this situation handled?

Are you willing to accept help from a Higher Power that could make your path easier and shorten the time to free you?

✦✦✦

If so, say this prayer or formulate one like it:

Great Spirit, I humbly ask You to do for me
what I cannot do for myself.

I am willing to accept the help I need,
and have this issue resolved quickly and easily,
by whatever means You deem most appropriate and effective.

Thank you, God, for Your guidance and Your grace.

MIRACULOUS MEETINGS

Stunned and inspired by my reading with Carla, I spent more time with her and I got to know her family. One day I received a phone call from Carla's daughter Deborah, bubbling with delight. "You're not going to believe what happened!" she oozed. "Mom is channeling a new guide who is full of love and fun. Unlike George, this guide animates mom and she walks through the room, eyes open, interacting with people."

"How cool!" I replied. "What's the guide's name?"

Deborah laughed. "She told us, 'Mary—not the virgin.'"

Later that year Carla and Mary (not the virgin) came to present a seminar for a study group I worked with in New Jersey. During the weekend retreat, each participant took a turn in a "hot seat" in which Carla, under the guide's direction, coached us one-to-one. True to Deborah's description, Mary was a delightful spirit. When she came through, Carla become more buoyant, playful, and deeply compassionate, still retaining her light-hearted irreverence. While George had expressed himself a bit on the British stiff-upper-lip side,

Mary was soft, motherly, and full of heart. I immediately felt safe with Mary and I savored being in her presence.

When my turn came to sit in the hot seat, Carla (under Mary's guidance) took me back in time to recall various defining moments in my life. Finally she directed me, "Go to the week between Christmas and New Year last year." The moment she mentioned that period, I burst into tears. That was the week my mother was dying. On Christmas Day, mom was ordered to leave the hospital because they could do no more for her, and I took her home to care for her. That week was hell for me. My mother withdrew more from her body daily, gradually losing her physical functions. Finally, on the day before New Year's Eve, she took a breath in, she breathed out, and did not breathe in again. I was very close with my mother, and part of me never expected her to die. But she did.

In the four months since my mother's passing, I had not allowed myself to grieve. I simply pushed on with my life, hiding in busyness and travels. Yet the loss and sorrow I felt pained me deeply behind my calm presentation. When Carla called my attention to that very difficult week, it tapped me into all the unresolved pain I had felt watching my mother wither and die. When I connected with my repressed pool of tears, I broke down. I had withdrawn my finger from the hole in the dike, and the ocean burst forth. I have never wept so deeply or long in my life, let alone in public. The people in the group were very patient and supportive, and allowed me the space to release. When I was finished, I felt deeply cleansed. I had made a major step toward coming out on the other side of my grieving process.

Toward the end of the seminar, Mary had a brief interaction with each person in the group. One fact I had never told her, or anyone, was that many people over the course of my life have mistakenly called me "David." Out of the blue, people would occasionally address me by that name and then apologize, "Gosh, I don't know where that came from." During my moment with Mary, she looked into my eyes and told me, "Your name was once David."

Postmark Heaven

At the time my mother passed, she had a *mezuzah,* a religious ritual object Jewish people fix on the doorpost of their homes. About the size of an index finger, the mezuzah contains a parchment from the Torah, and serves as a blessing to those who enter or leave the house.

My mom had asked me to post the mezuzah on the doorpost of her apartment, but because the frame was made of metal, it fell off. I glued it again, and again it came down. After several more failed attempts, the mezuzah ended up in her kitchen drawer until she passed away.

Six months later I received a phone call from Carla. "Did you get the present from your mom yet?"

Uh, I don't think so.

"You will," Carla told me with a giggle. "I was in a gift shop in St. Louis and your mom whispered in my ear to get you a present. Watch the mail."

A few days later a small package arrived. When I opened it, I was stunned to find a mezuzah similar to the one that had fallen down at my mom's house. I had not told Carla or anyone the mezuzah story, and she had no way of knowing about it.

Quickly I posted the mezuzah on the doorpost of my home, this time making sure it would not come down. How much more of a sign did I need?

Besides the amazing psychic feat behind the gift, one more lesson was obvious: *Even death cannot stop a Jewish mother.*

The Truth about Ancient Egypt

When the King Tut exhibit came to a Dallas museum, Carla and a group of her friends went to see it. While the group was wandering through the building, Mary "popped in." This was one of the most fascinating phenomena of Carla's channeling—sometimes fun and sometimes jarring. Occasionally Mary would just show up and animate Carla without any notice. Carla would be going about her life one moment, then lose all awareness of herself, and open her eyes minutes or hours later in a place entirely different from the one she had left! Carla never complained about this takeover nor felt possessed. On a soul level she had made an agreement with Mary that she could show up whenever it would be helpful.

When Mary popped in at the museum, she began to comment on the items on display. She had either had a lifetime or more in Egypt, or she was channeling information about the culture. She was quite familiar with the artifacts shown. Mary explained to the group what each item was used for, sometimes agreeing with the written description accompanying the item, and sometimes not. Regarding several artifacts, she noted, "This is not what they say it is, and it did not belong to that period."

After a while, other patrons of the exhibit began to join Mary and the gathered group, listening intently to the lecture. Since Mary was working through Carla, she looked like a normal person, and the unknowing onlookers assumed this was a genuine tour guide!

Little did they know how genuine it was.

An Unnecessary Phone Bill

Eventually Mary learned to use the telephone. Occasionally she would phone students who needed help and give them a few words of advice. She would simply pick up the receiver and psychically dial without touching the keypad. Yet the call would go through to the recipient.

While one of Mary's students was traveling cross country, she stopped to stay at a motel somewhere in the Midwest. To her surprise and delight, that night she received a telephone call from Mary, who gave her some important guidance. The woman had told no one she was at that motel. Mary just knew where to find and contact her.

Carla's husband Richard and other family members watched this process of psychic dialing in awe. When Richard checked the phone bills at the end of the month, Mary's calls were not listed or charged. After a while Richard, in his zeal to be helpful, decided to teach Mary how to dial the telephone. From that point on, the toll calls showed up on the bills. Richard's intervention proved to be a little too helpful!

Accelerated Healing

Over time, Deborah passed along to me amazing reports of the ways that Carla's guides helped her clients. One was a psychotherapist who consulted with the guides on his cases. (Carla explained that although one guide spoke through her at a time, there was a consortium of spirit guides from whom she received information.) The psychologist would phone Mary regularly and simply state, "Case 347," for example. With no further information, the guides would give him a detailed analysis of each case and offer specific recommendations for direction in treatment. The psychotherapist followed the guides' suggestions and obtained phenomenal results, accelerating his clients' progress in profound ways.

Prophecy and Providence

Soon after I met Mary I moved to Maui, where I shared a house with a few friends. The home was situated at an extraordinary location high on the slope of the sacred dormant volcano Haleakala, with a staggering view of the western shore of Maui, three other Hawaiian Islands, and jaw-dropping sunsets. The place was so heavenly that we hardly left it. What could be more enticing?

While I was living there, I had a reading with Mary, and I mentioned how much I enjoyed the place. She smiled and told me, "You will find an even nicer place." The prophecy puzzled me, since I could not even imagine a nicer place, and I was not looking for one.

A few months later, a friend brought a newspaper into the house—a rare event. As I casually paged through the paper, I came to the real estate section, where the entire front page was splashed with an ad for a property with the headline, "**This is it!!!!**"

Below the headline I found a description of a home in a rural section of Maui, on a hillside in the rainforest, with 360-degree views including ocean and mountains. The most stunning feature was a private waterfall on the property. My partner at the time, Karren, read the ad with me. "Let's look at it!" she suggested. I was all ears.

Karren and I went to look at the property, which was indeed magnificent and even more heavenly than the home I shared with my friends. We made a deal on the spot and moved in a few months later. This was one of the most impulsive things I have ever done, yet the most successful.

The house served as my haven for 26 years, where I found magnificent inspiration, wrote many books, and felt healed in the natural setting.

We may pray for things we think we need, or settle for things we believe are in our best interest, while the object we are praying for is not right for us, or something better may be in store. We may be tempted to try to force a particular result, or cling to a situation that is more of a stepping stone than a landing place. In all cases we do best to turn our life over to Higher Power, trusting that It knows how to provide for us more efficiently than we know how to provide for ourselves. When we surrender our human will to God's will, miracles happen.

DIRECT CONNECT 5
This or Better

In each of the following areas, check the box that describes your experience at the moment:

Area	Miserable, I can't stand it anymore	Pretty unhappy, but putting up with it	Okay, but could be better	Pretty good, but could be even better	Really good, I can't imagine better
My body & health					
My primary relationship					
My family					
My job					
My finances					
My home & living situation					
My friendships					
My religion or spiritual path					
Other:					

In each situation, what change would represent a happy, healthy improvement?

> In situations you can't imagine being better, are you open
> to the universe delivering to you even better?
>
> ✳ ✳ ✳
>
> Offer this prayer or one like it of your own choosing:
>
> **Great Spirit, please guide me to**
> **what will be best for me and everyone involved.**
>
> **I trust that You know my best interests and**
> **You will bring me what will make me the happiest.**
>
> **And so it is.**

What a Wise Person Would Do

Mary's prediction about the home was the first of many events she prophesied. While occasionally some of her predictions did not manifest, she was generally quite accurate. For example, I was scheduled to lead a pilgrimage to the sacred sites of Egypt in the fall of 1990. During spring of that year I asked Mary what she thought about the idea. She told me, "There will be some events occurring this summer, we believe around August, that will affect the trip." I was mystified by her comment, but I just let it go and waited to see what would happen.

On August 2, 1990, news arrived that the Iraqi army had invaded Kuwait, which set off a chain of events we all now recognize. Soon America and other countries sent in troops to combat the Iraqis. War had broken out in the Middle East. The organizers of our seminar and I struggled with the decision of whether or not to go ahead with the trip to Egypt. When I asked Mary for her advice, she simply answered, "One who was wise would not go."

I had to laugh when Mary spoke this. She never leveraged pressure or dogmatic instructions, always honoring my right and responsibility to make my own decisions. She gave hints and suggestions, and the rest was up to me. After sitting with her idea for a while, I decided to be one who was wise. We cancelled the trip for that year but resurrected it years later after the political situation had settled down.

How psychics and prophets can predict future events is a mystery from the human standpoint. Yet we can understand such expanded vision from a spiritual perspective. Mary once offered the analogy of the difference between driving a car on the freeway and seeing the freeway from a helicopter's vantage point. If you are stuck in traffic, you are limited to a two-dimensional view. You don't know why the traffic is jammed, how far ahead it is congested, or where or when you might find an exit ramp to take another route. From the helicopter's view, you can see the bigger picture and make an accurate assessment of how to navigate. Mary's prediction of my new home and the war in the Middle East proved to be cogent demonstrations that there is a higher way of knowing that can help us in important ways when we tap into it.

A Portal to a Higher Dimension

When Mary conducted a class for a group, she lifted the room to a higher, finer frequency, as if taking us on a magic carpet to tour a blissful kingdom. While our bodies remained sitting on chairs, we were transported far beyond the physical space. Mary seemed to turn a dial, and suddenly we were absorbed in deep abiding peace, like a warm, soothing bath.

If you have ever had such an uplifting experience, or studied with someone who can activate a dimensional shift, you are blessed. Ultimately you don't need anyone to achieve this for you, although if someone can, you do well to take advantage of the opportunity. Once you have had a taste of heaven, the earth plane loses its allure; when you know there is more, you are no longer willing to settle for less. The goal of the spiritual path is to keep ascending to higher ground. The knowledge of heaven is your birthright and destiny because the knowledge of heaven is knowledge of yourself.

The Door Swings Both Ways

Carla Gordan passed away in September 2003. Her departure was felt deeply by the many who loved her and the teachings she generously shared. Yet Carla left a legacy of wisdom that remains to nourish those seeking answers from a higher source. (To access books, audios, and teachings by Carla and the guides, visit www.carlaneffgordan.com.)

In the years prior to her passing, Carla dealt with a number of health difficulties. One worth noting involved a diagnosis Carla's doctor gave her when she was having fainting spells. The physician told her, "There is a mechanism in the brain that alerts the body when a person begins to die. That mechanism sounds an alarm to the entire body to marshal its energies to survive. For some reason, that mechanism in your brain is not functioning as it should."

The diagnosis is significant because Carla exited her body almost daily for thirty-five years. When Carla gave readings and taught channeled classes, she would step out of the consciousness of her body and allow her spirit guides to animate her for the purpose of teaching. In a way, she "died" daily, leaving her body often and then reentering. It is no wonder, then, that the mechanism that alerted the body to imminent death had been disabled or was perhaps used so much by the door swinging both ways that it "came off the hinges." Ultimately this was not the cause of her death, but the phenomenon is quite relevant to the work she did.

How a Real Teacher Teaches

I saw Mary for a reading several times a year for nearly two decades, during which she, Carla, and the guides gave me feedback on my spiritual progress, answered questions about crucial issues in my life, helped me make important decisions, and affirmed my worth and my connection to the Source of all life and love.

The most valuable gift Mary gave me, among so many, was self-empowerment. When I sat with her, I never felt that I was with someone closer to God than me. To the contrary, when Mary gave me advice or her perspective on the subjects I asked about, I felt that she was confirming my own inner knowing that I had yet to trust. I realized that my intuition had been guiding me all along, but I was not listening to it. In essence, Mary helped me build a bridge to my higher self. This was far more helpful than if she had fostered a need for her. To remain dependent on an external source to tell you how to live only weakens you. To know that you have access to all the wisdom you will ever need, directly from your soul, is the greatest blessing a teacher can impart.

DIRECT CONNECT 6
Empowered Guidance

If you are studying with a psychic, healer, medium, teacher, or therapist:

In what ways does this healer foster your dependence on him or her?

In what ways does this healer empower you to be independent?

Do you realize that you have access to the wisdom you seek through this person?

Do you in any way give your power away to this person? If so, how?

If you were to take your power back, how would you be relating to this person differently?

What choices would you be making for yourself with or without this person's guidance?

How much, and in what ways, has this guide empowered you to recognize your own wisdom, strength, and wholeness?

If you are a teacher or healer, do you seek to empower your students' or clients' independence?

Are there any ways you could empower your students or clients more?

Walking the Talk

Beyond her extraordinary gifts as a medium, Carla Gordan was an exemplary teacher in her own right, deeply dedicated to healing and service to humanity. She didn't seek fame, power, or lavish wealth. (Some of the best healers do not become well-known; they simply serve humbly and quietly and allow the universe to connect them with the people they can most help.) When I visited the room in Carla's home where she conducted readings via telephone, I noticed a small slip of paper taped onto the back of the receiver. It reminded her to consistently ask, *"How can I help?"*

I once invited Carla to speak at a large conference I organized, where many different teachers offered lectures. One of the teachers reported that someone had stolen his cash box from his vending booth in the hotel lobby. The fellow was quite upset. Hearing that news, Carla offered to give a few extra readings at the conference and donate the proceeds to offset his deficit. To me this served as a teaching that grace has the power to supersede karma.

All I felt from Carla and the guides was unconditional love. In my sessions with Mary, I revealed facts and questions about my path that I now recognize as signs that I was more unconscious or lost than I knew at the time. I made some foolish decisions I would not make now. Yet through all these processes I never felt judged or made wrong by Carla, Mary, or the guides. They simply accepted me exactly where I was, saw the best in me, and used their skills to bring forth my greater self. The more I have grown and matured, the more I appreciate the respect, blessing, and healing shown to me by these extraordinary teachers. As a result, I strive to bring the same quality of love to the people I now teach. I don't always succeed, but I have a shining role model that keeps me reaching for the highest integrity.

Still Here

In the years since Carla passed, I sometimes wish I could still meet with her and the guides she channeled. I miss their presence, profound insights, and remarkable guidance. I have rarely met other psychics or channelers who reach the same benchmark of excellence and soul guidance that I experienced with Carla and her crew.

Yet I have gained another kind of growth that in some ways supersedes having such a gifted healer in my physical presence. More and more, I can connect with Mary myself. When faced with a significant decision or troubling situation, I ask her for help. Usually I can hear her voice speaking to me in response. I know Mary's energy, her value system, and her intentions. So, while the body that channeled the spirit is gone, the spirit thrives. The entity that spoke through Carla continues to exist beyond the physical dimension. When I raise my consciousness to match the frequency of the guides, they are here. There is no time, space, or death in spirit, and they have not gone anywhere. Carla's passing pushed me out of the nest and forced me to fly with my own wings. There was an apparent loss in the physical world, but no loss in the spiritual dimension. The guides would be the first to teach that in God loss of any kind is impossible, and death is the shabbiest of illusions.

We all have help from above. Your guides are with you, and you can connect with them. To attract and avail yourself of the guides' help, live your life at the highest frequency possible. Each day cultivate your spiritual connection. Ask your Higher Power for help when you need it. Keep your mind and heart open, trust, extend kindness, exercise discernment, act with integrity, and everything you need will show up in perfect order and timing. Love knows where you live.

DIRECT CONNECT 7
Empowered Healing Relationships

Have you studied with a valued teacher, healer, or therapist who has passed on or otherwise left your life?

Do you ever miss that person and wish that he or she was still with you?

Can you tap into that person's energy field and access the wisdom and love they showed you?

✳ ✳ ✳

Try this practice:

Close your eyes, relax, breathe deeply, and get quiet. Call your guide to you by mentally focusing on their name, face, or energy. When you feel their presence, tell them what is going on in your life and ask for guidance. Be still and listen for their voice, energy, or some sign or symbol of a message helpful to you. Take your time and be open until you receive some wisdom. When you feel complete, open your eyes and write the message you received.

You can repeat this exercise whenever and as often as you like. Over time, you will develop your ability to connect with your guide(s) and access whatever you need to know.

TRANCE
ENCOUNTERS

Guide Mary never referred to Carla by her name. She called Carla "this body I wear." While the appellation was initially deflating to Carla (but later humorous), there was a teaching behind the term. In the channeling process, a spiritual being or group uses the channel as a kind of "telepathic telephone" to communicate with people in the physical world. A person who channels is a step-down transformer, taking lofty ideas from a higher-vibrational realm and translating them into terms the masses can hear and understand. While every human being has access to spirit guides, few people are attuned to connect with them or skilled at the process. So entities in spirit take the path of least resistance and speak through people who are open to serve as a bridge between worlds.

An authentic channel has a soul contract with the entity he or she brings through. This agreement was established before birth at a far deeper level than the human personality. When the moment is ripe in the channel's development, the guide shows up. All of the channels I mention in this book did not plan to channel or make any effort to do so. In all cases the entity entered their life by surprise. Yet as the relationship developed, the channel realized that it was but the human personality that was surprised. The process was no surprise to the soul, which had consciously collaborated with the entity seeking to communicate.

Many people wish to become channels and take classes or do exercises to develop their channeling faculties. Such practices can enhance an individual's psychic abilities and, if founded in healthy spiritual principles, improve the quality of the student's life and deliver wisdom to others. Yet in my experience, genuine channeling is a gift to be recognized more than a faculty to be developed. Such a profound relationship cannot be cultivated by the ego, intellect, or personality. It is not a career you choose. It chooses you. Mediumship is a destiny you have co-created with God. The people I have seen who try to become channels rarely attain the sublime state that naturally gifted channels demonstrate. Medium Matt Fraser said, "Anyone can learn to play the piano, but not everyone is destined to become a Beethoven or Mozart." This is not to discourage you from channeling and psychic development. We can all benefit from attuning more astutely to spiritual guidance. We all already channel more than we know. My intention in this book is to encourage you to find out what you came to channel and how you can connect with your higher self rather than traipsing through astral planes seeking entities to speak through you. People who go looking for entities usually get inferior ones, if they are real at all. Psychic abilities reveal themselves naturally as a byproduct of spiritual advancement. If you attempt to gain psychic powers before you reach commensurate spiritual growth, they won't do you any good. Focus on spiritual development, and all else, including psychic faculties, shall be added where helpful. Regardless of psychic manifestations, every human being has talents and passions to bring divinely inspired gifts to the world. Some people have the gift to channel specific entities, and others channel inspiring art, gardening, teaching, books, healing, mothering, or developing a business. Pray to live the life you uniquely came to live. The most important entity you can channel is yourself.

Everything in Due Time

If you are eager to receive channeled messages or any form of guidance from within, trust that the information most helpful to you will be delivered at the right and perfect time. Never try to rush or force an answer for yourself or someone else. Trust that your guide(s) know when and how guidance will be delivered to you for your highest benefit.

When Carla's daughter Deborah had not received any messages for a length of time, she asked the guides why there had been such a gap. They explained that in her last reading they had given her all the information she needed; now she needed to practice the teachings so they could sink into her soul and be real in her experience.

The same divine mind that knows what is best for you also knows when and how to tell you what you need to know. The spiritual path is not simply about accumulating information; it is about turning information into wisdom by putting it into practice in daily life.

The guides also explained to Carla that they showed up when she had elevated her energy to a point that matched the information the guides wished to impart. Authentic spiritual guidance operates at a particular frequency. To be a channel or receive higher information, you must be a vibrational match to the guides and the guidance.

Readers of the Lost Art

The individual who legitimized channeling during the past century was Edgar Cayce, "the sleeping prophet." Born in 1877 on a Kentucky farm, as a child Cayce demonstrated extraordinary psychic abilities such as observing auras, seeing angels, conversing with departed spirits, prescribing accurate cures for illnesses, and being able to learn lessons from his schoolbooks while sleeping with his head on a book. As a young man, Cayce contracted severe laryngitis and lost his voice entirely for a year. No doctor was able to cure him. Then a hypnotist offered to treat him. While in a trance, Cayce followed the instruction of a spirit guide and prescribed a cure for his ailment, which worked. Cayce then discovered that he could induce a trance, during which he accurately diagnosed the illnesses of people who came to him in person or at a distance, and prescribed effective cures.

Word of Cayce's gifts spread rapidly, and before long many people were coming to Cayce for soul readings, which included overviews of their past lives as well as guidance for their current life. He also spoke in detail about the ancient civilizations of Atlantis and Egypt, and the history of the world. Considering his readings a gift from God, Cayce did not charge for them, but subsisted on donations. Over the course of his lifetime, Cayce conducted over 14,000 readings with remarkable accuracy. His readings are well documented and freely available to the public online and in bound volumes at the Association for Research and Enlightenment, the organization established by Cayce in Virginia Beach, which continues to proliferate his work. (www.edgarcayce.org)

A more contemporary respected exponent of nonphysical reality is Dr. Brian Weiss, a psychiatrist who has devoted much of his life to the study and teaching of past life regression, reincarnation, and the immortality of the soul. While

Dr. Weiss was Head of Psychiatry at Mount Sinai Medical Center in Miami, he was treating a particularly difficult client who did not respond to traditional psychiatric methods. As a last resort, Dr. Weiss tried a hypnotic age regression. The psychiatrist was astounded when his patient did not stop her regression at her childhood, but continued to move back in time and describe her previous lives and the intervals between them. Dr. Weiss was intrigued, but skeptical. His doubting dissolved when the spirit entity who spoke through his patient gave the doctor personal information about his life that she could not possibly have known. Several years before that encounter, Dr. Weiss and his wife had a child who passed away at a young age. A tender personal memory, the Weisses did not make knowledge of this event available to the public. During this regression, the patient gave Dr. Weiss extraordinarily accurate information about the child and his death. This stunning experience gave Dr. Weiss a strong belief and faith in the process of channeling, reincarnation, and the spirit world. Brian Weiss recounted his discoveries in his bestselling book *Many Lives, Many Masters*, and continues to explore and teach about reincarnation and how to access information about the nonphysical dimension. (www.brianweiss.com)

I cite these two well-known teachers as compelling examples of legitimate purveyors of spiritual communication. Their credentials, documentation, and results are impeccable. Any sincere exploration of their work must yield an understanding that there is a vast dimension of spirit that we can tap into to gain wisdom and peace of mind in an otherwise confusing and often daunting world.

DIRECT CONNECT 8
Glimmers of Higher Dimensions

Have you had any moments of revelation in which you caught a glimpse of a higher dimension, such as through a dream, psychic insight, past life memory, vision, or near-death experience?

If so, what did you see, know, or sense during that moment of illumination?

How has that experience affected and uplifted your normal waking life?

Have you been able to tap into or recapture that moment, or one like it, to gain inspiration when you need it?

What can you do to encourage such insights to come to you?

Do you have faith in what you saw or knew, and trust that this experience was given by God to uplift your life, heal you, and encourage you to share this knowledge to inspire and comfort others?

A SPIN AROUND THE CAMPUS

Every profession includes practitioners dedicated to serving their clients, and others who lack integrity. The realm of channeling and psychic guidance is no exception. There are masterful mediums, mediocre messengers, and dangerous deliverers. Let's take a quick tour of the world of spiritual guidance, so that you may recognize where any channel stands on the continuum of integrity, and how you can most effectively benefit from studying with one.

The Truly Gifted

Some channels, mediums, and psychics are pure of heart, noble of intention, and genuinely gifted. They tap into the highest source and deliver precise, healing, life-transforming messages. Divine light shines bright and strong through a clean, clear window. Such teachers' profound insights offer specific personal guidance relevant to your spiritual and earthly journey. If you find such a teacher, you are blessed. God is speaking through that person. In their presence a portal to heaven opens, and you feel that you have come home. If you put their teachings into practice, you will find soul satisfaction and your material life will unfold in wonderful ways. No greater gift can be given. I thank God for the transformational insights and healing I have received from authentic channels. Their presence on Earth is an act of grace, their service to humanity paramount.

Gifted but Compromised

Some channels are genuinely gifted, but they are distracted by ego or personality frailties. As a result, their transmissions become diluted, a mishmash of truth and illusions. They may tap into information or guidance from a higher power, even distinct nonphysical entities, but by the time the lessons reach the student they may be watered down or distorted by the channel's biases, fears, confused intentions, or personal dramas.

If a ray of pure light passes through a dusty or dirty window, some or much of the light will be obscured, and the room it falls upon will reveal a mixture of light and shadows. If the light passes through stained glass, you will see light in the shade the glass is colored. In some cases, the images may be fascinating, innocuous, and even entertaining. Stained glass windows are glorious because the coloring is creative, attractive, and uplifting. So a message filtered through an interesting personality can make the transmission endearing. If the window is dirty or warped, light will be blocked or scattered in a distorted pattern, and the patterns that appear in the room will misrepresent the original light that reached the window.

Working with a compromised channel can be tricky. As a student, part of you stirs at the recognition of truth, but then you must sift out the falsehoods. Master teacher Ram Dass recounted the parable of a renowned soothsayer who confessed to his disciples, "I find myself in a most difficult predicament. Years ago I was put under a spell by a wizard. As a result, some of what I tell you is pure truth from God. If you apply these teachings, your soul will come to peace and you will be liberated. Other elements of my teachings are mired in error and delusion. If you follow them, your life will be a sorry mess. My dilemma is that I don't know which elements are true and which are lies."

The story gets up close and personal because it applies to every teacher walking the Earth, including psychics, channelers, mediums, gurus, therapists, and self-help teachers. Even the best teachers have some gaps or distortion in the information they transmit. If you believe that every word that proceeds from a channeler's lips is the infallible word of God, you may be misexercising faith. Real faith means that you have one hundred percent trust in God, not a person. It also means that you trust your inner guidance that shows you how to discern truth from falsehood. Some teachings will resonate with a big "Yes!" in your soul. Others will fall flat or grate against your soul. If something does not feel right, it is not right, at least for you. "Maybe wrong, maybe not for me, maybe later." Trust your guidance, and do not allow a lack of self-confidence to override your inner guru. As the German philosopher Wolfgang von Goethe advised, "As soon as you trust yourself, you will know how to live."

Well-intentioned but Not Necessarily Gifted

I have heard a number of channelers deliver very pure and loving messages, but as far as I can tell, they are not connected to any unique entity or source of guidance. Such lovely people with good hearts sincerely seek to live in the light, share wisdom, and uplift the world. For those reasons they are worth listening to and putting their teachings into practice. But they are more uttering broad-stroke spiritual principles and platitudes than channeling an entity. They guide students to follow your heart; know that you are embraced by God; accept abundance; forgive yourself; live in harmony with one another and nature; and more. All of these teachings are absolutely true and important to follow. Such teachers deserve our attention and practice of their teachings. Yet when it comes to unique answers specific to the asker, or direct guidance, the channel does not deliver. Instead, they utter blanket truths that can apply to anyone. If you have ever sat with someone who is channeling a specific entity connected to truth, you know that the entity generates a commanding presence and guides students uniquely, personally, and directly. A channel who delivers broad-stroke spiritual truths does not do that.

If you have a choice between working with a well-intentioned but not necessarily gifted channel and one who is gifted but compromised, you will do better to take the more general path and avoid the pitfalls of a distracted guide. Truth works not because it comes from a particular entity, but because you put it into action. You can get enlightened with a false teacher because you put the principles he utters into practice, even if the teacher does not practice them himself. Yet if you can find a pure channel, you will accelerate faster than in any other teaching relationship.

Wannabes

Some channelers are not connected to any authentic source of wisdom. They may believe they are qualified and present themselves as such, but they are not. They may be enamored with the idea of channeling, or like the idea of earning income from the profession, or seek the limelight. But the material that comes through is not channeled. They have not been well trained and they do not have the soul maturity to be truly helpful. They may toss around spiritual catch phrases, but because they are not aligned with truth, their teachings are relatively impotent.

Anyone can say they are channeling, and they may attract students who are impressed. There is a certain reconciliation in situations where unqualified teachers attract naïve students: both are at the same level of learning and match each other. There are lessons here for all involved. While it is possible to learn from an unqualified teacher, you will do far better to work with someone who is connected to authentic wisdom.

Charlatans

A small percentage of channelers know full well that that they are not channeling, but seek to exploit people seeking help. Or they chase money, power, fame, attention, or sex. Think of the types of channelers plotted on a bell curve. At one end there are a small number who are truly gifted. In the middle are teachers with moderate talent or integrity. At the other end of the curve are a few outright frauds. Evil—ignorance or illusion—has a way of creeping into every domain; religion and spirituality are among its favorite targets.

The fact that the realm of channelers contains a few bad apples does not disqualify the real ones. Just because you can fake something does not mean that the genuine is fake too. A handful of bad doctors should not stop people from seeing the many good ones. It is easy for skeptics and cynics to point to fraudulent channelers as a justification to discredit the profession. Yet every profession contains individuals who taint it. They also contain professionals who help many people and bless the world.

Let the buyer beware. If something stinks, there is something rotten in Denmark. A real teacher stands the test of noble character and positive results. "By their fruits you shall know them." If your teacher has integrity, is truly helping people, and lives a life worth emulating, stick with him or her. If a teacher falls short of character, kindness, or positive results, exit stage left.

DIRECT CONNECT 9

Identifying Integrity

If you have studied with a spiritual teacher, psychic, medium, or channeler, note where you believe this person stands on the continuum of integrity.

Name	Truly gifted	Gifted but compromised	Well-intentioned but not gifted	Wannabe	Charlatan

For those other than the truly gifted:

What have you learned or can you learn from your relationship with this person?

How has this person helped you gain discernment on your

---

spiritual path?

How has this person helped you look into your own character or teachings, that you may improve them?

Can you thank and bless *all* of your teachers for the life lessons you have gained from studying with them?

✦ ✦ ✦

Say this prayer/affirmation or formulate your own:

Thank you, God, for all of my teachers, including the pure and the impure. You have sent me all of them for my spiritual growth. Some teach me what to do, and others teach me what not to do. I bless all of my teaching relationships, I am grateful for them, and I use what I have learned to advance on my path.

Guidance, Direction, and Discernment

Never before have so many spiritual teachings been available to so many. The Internet has expanded our learning opportunities exponentially. Not very long ago, esoteric teachings were available only to a handful of people. To sit in the presence of a spiritual master, you had to travel to distant lands and overcome all kinds of obstacles and initiations. Now you can sit in your living room, press a few buttons, and find the secret teachings of all ages. What an amazing time we live in!

Yet with the multiplicity of quality teachings come elements of illusion and deception. For this reason we must exercise wisdom, maturity, and discernment when choosing a channeler or spiritual teacher. You can strengthen your ability to connect with a qualified teacher by praying for guidance and direction. Ask sincerely, and your prayer will be answered.

DIRECT CONNECT 10

Pray for Right Teachings

If you are seeking a teacher or higher teachings, pray:

Great Spirit, please connect me with a teacher who is pure of heart, gifted in wisdom, and can help me advance on my spiritual path. Reveal to me who can support me most effectively. Give me the guidance and discernment to choose wisely. I am open and willing to receive healthy guidance to improve the quality of my life and be of service to others. By the Grace of God, so it is.

After you have sincerely uttered this prayer or one like it, get on with your life. Live your daily activities at the highest octave you can touch. Be more concerned with practicing the teachings you have been given rather than finding someone to give you more teachings. You have already received many jewels. To graduate to the next level, master the principles you have been shown. At this moment you have within you all that you need to live the best life you can imagine. Searching for an outer teacher can be a denial or distraction from connecting with your inner teacher. As you exercise your internal guidance, you can save years or lifetimes of seeking someone to tell you how to live.

If there is someone in the outer world who can help you, he or she will show up with the least effort and no struggle on your part. Grace has your back. The adage "when the student is ready, the teacher appears" is absolutely true. My most important teachers have simply shown up in the natural course of me walking my path, sometimes when I least expected them. Likewise, your teachers will find you.

If you feel desperate to find a teacher or a channeled entity to guide you, you will attract desperate results. God knows your needs. If you really need help, it will come naturally and organically. Develop your relationship with God, who lives in your heart, and all of your earthly teachers and relationships will arrange themselves in miraculous ways. You are loved, you are guided, and you are worthy to have all the teachings you need to take you all the way home.

PART III

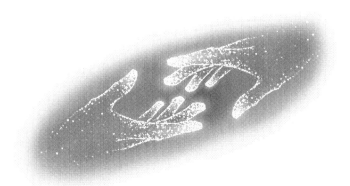

HILDA AND THE MASTERS:

MIGHTY COMPANIONS

THE TEACHER APPEARS

As I entered the hall packed with spiritual seekers, I had no idea how that evening's meeting would change my life. A friend had invited me to Hilda Charlton's class held in a large gym on the grounds of St. Luke's Church in lower Manhattan. There I found hundreds of students sitting cross-legged on the floor and tables, in the rafters, and anywhere a body could be wedged. Some were meditating, little pictures of gurus at their feet beside burning sticks of incense. An air of anticipation filled the space.

Soon a grandmotherly woman wearing an elegant white Indian *sari* entered. Her dark medium-length hair set off a strong-featured face with deep-set eyes. The students cleared a path for the teacher as she coasted gracefully with a dignified, self-assured air. Hilda smiled kindly, nodded, and made eye contact with those she passed. She was accompanied by an attractive young woman carrying a guitar.

Hilda took a seat at the front of the room, and the guitarist, Mirabai, offered several songs to warm up the audience. Mirabai's voice rang bold on upbeat rock songs, and then modulated to velvet smoothness on softer melodies. After thirty minutes, when Hilda sensed the energy was ripe, she rose and spoke. She began with some funny stories that loosened the clenched New York crowd, who had arrived on the heels of a stressful day at work. The music soothed our emotions and made us receptive to the lesson that followed. Then came the jewel of the evening, a "message from the masters." Hilda explained that she was awakened regularly at 3:00 a.m., when a spiritual guide dictated instructions on how to live masterfully. During that quiet time, Hilda took pen to paper and diligently recorded every precious word. Then she would transmit the message to our class on the following Thursday evening. Tonight's lesson was on the importance of choosing healing words. God has given us the power to create through our speech, and we must be careful to speak positive, uplifting, soul-nourishing words rather than drag ourselves and others down with negative, critical, or careless speech.

The class concluded with a guided meditation that transported me to a magical, soul-soothing realm. Like Guide Mary, Hilda was gifted with a unique power to lift a gathering to a lofty etheric dimension. She unlocked a portal to heaven, and gracefully took us with her. All of the elements of the class—from the opening music, to the humor, to the lecture—were preludes to the rarified moments when we met God face-to-face. The meditation healed at the deepest level of soul. When the inner journey was complete, Mirabai segued with a soulful ballad that sounded like a love song to a person, but was really directed to God. By the time the song landed me gently back in the meeting hall, I was changed.

When I fell into bed that night, I was enfolded in deep serenity. The experience was not dramatic, but rather crept into my soul like the aroma of sweet incense. When I awoke the next morning, I felt extraordinarily clear and alive, as if my mind and heart had been cleansed and healed, setting me on track with my purpose.

The next week I returned to Hilda's class, and the next, and the next. This unusual teacher had no organization, membership, mailing list, admission fee, dues, products to sell, or obligation of any kind. She just showed up and gave her gift, and those who recognized its value met her there. Without planning or forethought, I went week after week for fourteen years, hardly ever missing a class. Nothing was more important than what I was learning from my mentor. During that period, my life shifted in quantum ways, setting me firmly on the spiritual path. In my college years I had been immersed in social drinking, smoking weed and cigarettes, and undiscerning dating. After meeting Hilda, all of those indulgences gradually fell away; in contrast to the lightness and freedom I felt under her tutelage, those habits seemed dense and weighty, and I simply lost interest in them. Why settle for cut glass when a diamond was offered? Hilda gave me an unsurpassed foundation in values and practices that create a meaningful life. She was a friend, guru, teacher, disciplinarian, mother, and mentor to me and thousands of others whose lives were transformed by her loving presence. I cannot overestimate the value of the gifts this unusual holy woman bestowed upon me and so many. I am and will be forever grateful.

Stage 3 of Spiritual Evolution

When you are ripe, you attract a physical mentor. This person answers your deeper questions, helps you make decisions at crucial crossroads, and becomes a role model you aspire to emulate. The student is ready, the teacher appears, and you enjoy a solid connection with one you can turn to for answers and support. This teaching relationship continues and deepens over time, bearing soul-nourishing fruit for student and teacher.

The Guru Appears

As a young girl growing up in Salt Lake City in the 1920's, Hilda had many other-worldly experiences. When she prayed and meditated in her bedroom, various angels, saints, and even Jesus Christ appeared and spoke directly to her. The oddest apparition was that of a dark-skinned Indian yogi sitting under a palm tree. The mystic had a large belly and wore only a small loincloth. He spoke no words, but simply made a pointing gesture with his thumb and grunted. Hilda did not know what to make of this strange vision, but she felt a strong connection with the being she beheld.

At that time in America, there was very little interest or understanding of mysticism, yoga, or spirituality. Now there are countless books, classes, seminars, gurus, ashrams, and online courses. In Hilda's era, people who had visions or talked about nonphysical existence were branded weirdos; just a few spiritual teachers were bold enough to step into the public eye. So this girl with higher vision had to forge her own path and develop her unique relationship with her guides and God.

Hilda became a classical dancer and crafted interpretive dances to celebrate various esoteric traditions. She created the Dance of St. Francis, the Dance of Angkor Wat, and the Dance of the Mayan Priestess. Her talent, grace, and vibrant presence earned her acclaim as she performed in prestigious venues, including the Hollywood Bowl. She spent personal time with the legendary Paramahansa Yogananda, beloved author of the classic text *Autobiography of a Yogi*.

In the late 1940's Hilda travelled with a dance troupe to India, where she planned to stay for six months. When she arrived in that land of ancient spirituality, Hilda felt as if she had come home. She adopted the lifestyle of a renunciate, trekked barefoot on long pilgrimages, climbed to remote caves in the Himalayas, and studied with renowned yogis, including Satya Sai Baba, who welcomed Hilda to dwell in his residence for eighteen months. During her travels, Hilda met many spiritual masters who healed, performed miracles, and accelerated their disciples' enlightenment.

At one point Hilda heard about a revered yogi named Sri Nityananda. Curious, she traveled to the master's ashram, where she was astounded to behold the very same loincloth-clad yogi who had visited her in her childhood apparition! True to Hilda's vision, Nityananda remained silent, making the same gesture with his thumb while grunting. Something inside Hilda thrilled to sit in that master's presence. "In that moment I knew I had met my true guru," she recounted.

The six months in India gave way to eighteen years, until in the mid-1960's Hilda had to return to New York to do some paperwork regarding her visa. She planned to stay in the U.S. for just a few weeks, but when she arrived she discovered that the world she was returning to was not the one she had left. "A consciousness revolution was taking place in America," Hilda recalled. "So many young people were hungry for knowledge of spiritual dimensions. I was amazed!"

A few seekers found Hilda and discovered she had answers to their spiritual questions they had not been able to satisfy elsewhere. These students brought their friends to meet her, so she started a small weekly class in her apartment. When the group outgrew the apartment, it moved to a larger venue, and then to the gym on the grounds of St. Luke's Church in Greenwich Village. Later the class expanded to the huge sanctuary of the magnificent Cathedral of St. John the Divine, where Hilda's lessons found their way to the hearts of thousands who sought healing and guidance.

The students were ready. The teacher appeared.

DIRECT CONNECT 11
The Teacher Appears

Considering the important teachers, mentors, and healers who have helped you:

Who has shown up as a result of your own efforts or manipulation?

Who has shown up by divine orchestration and synchronicity?

How did your best teachers appear with impeccable timing to help you where you stood at that moment?

If you are seeking a teacher or guidance now, can you trust that your teacher will appear in the perfect way and timing to help you in the way you can most benefit?

✳ ✳ ✳

Speak this affirmation or one like it:

I am grateful for the divine timing and synchronicity with which my most valued teachers have come into my life. I trust that as I continue my spiritual journey, all the right teachers and guidance will find me in the perfect way and timing.

A UNIVERSITY BEYOND TIME

The initial messages Hilda transmitted were from The Great White Brotherhood*, a group of ascended masters who live in a spiritual dimension and are dedicated to the upliftment of humanity. Some of the masters she introduced were Master Hilarion, Master Count St. Germain, and Master El Morye. Their lessons implored us to live our divine purpose, hold a pure vibration, not be daunted by challenges, and serve humankind. When Hilda read those noble messages, I felt a rarified energy, distinctly different from the tone of her regular voice and teaching. I felt as if my atomic structure was being rearranged for the better. I did not simply learn facts about the ascended masters, I sat in their presence.

---

*The term "White Brotherhood" does not refer to physical race. The Brotherhood is comprised of spiritual masters of many different races, including male and female entities. The term "white" in this case refers to a particular frequency of pure energy, like white light. When Carla Gordan began channeling, the guides also introduced themselves as members of the Great White Brotherhood. Carla had never heard that term before.

Over time, Hilda introduced us to many different spiritual beings who visited her in the cloistered silence of those mystic hours. She explained that the middle of the night, around 3:00 to 4:00 a.m., is the time of the masters, when beings from a higher plane can easily reach humanity to deliver guidance and healing. During that period, the psychic activity and distractions of the world are at a minimum, providing an optimum window for spiritual aspirants to meditate, pray, receive and develop creative ideas, or, as she did, take dictation from the realm of spirit. If you are awakened during that time, Hilda advised, take advantage of the energy and engage in any spiritually uplifting activity.

Some of the angelic beings who appeared to Hilda and gave her messages included Mother Mary, St. Theresa of Lisieux, St. Joan of Arc, St. Martin de Porres, the Hindu god Skanda, George Washington Carver, and notable individuals from many religions and spiritual traditions, as well as secular leaders. When Hilda received a message from the Greek statesman Pericles, she devoted numerous classes to introduce her students to this dignified personage. As Hilda recounted his noble achievements to advance democracy, architecture, and culture, she captured and transmitted his passion, mission, and legacy. We walked side by side with the prominent orator and general, conversed with him intimately, and saw the world through his eyes. During the Pericles lessons I realized that by opening myself to Hilda's rare form of teaching I had enrolled in a kind of university beyond time, in which I was transported to meet and learn from some of the greatest minds and hearts in all of history.

One evening Hilda announced that she had been visited by Chief Red Cloud, a Native American who had fought valiantly for the cause of his people when settlers were attempting to dislodge them from their land. Red Cloud pleaded for the plight of Native Americans in his time and ours. While I had learned a bit in school about the history of Native Americans, I gained a deeper compassionate understanding of their plight. Hilda's meeting with that spiritual leader led to a connection with Chief Joseph of the Nez Perce, and others. During that year, our class immersed ourselves in the world of Native Americans, took field trips to modern pow-wows, and participated in traditional dances and ceremonies with the culture we came to respect and support.

Then Hilda revealed that she had been visited by several "space brothers" who represented extraterrestrial civilizations attempting to contact and help Earth. The months that ensued brought many UFO sightings by members of our group, along with guided meditations to raise our vibration and establish energetic contact with galactic cultures advanced far beyond our own. The energy of the E.T. transmissions was not at all related to the titillating or frightening accounts often associated with the phenomenon in pop culture; instead, it was founded on the principle that all living beings, in this world and beyond, are expressions of one God, the source of all life. We must join together to advance the evolution of consciousness for all beings in all dimensions.

All of the teachings of Hilda's friends in high places came to me not by intellect, but by direct experience. Whatever Hilda taught, we felt. We did not simply believe in her spiritual comrades; we knew them. I have never met another individual who had the power to transport souls to such a variety of dimensions and connect with so many different illumined entities. Our teacher was truly a cosmic tour guide.

What was in it for Hilda? Was she making money on the channeling, building an empire, gathering followers, or on an ego trip? None of the above. Hilda never charged a penny for any of her classes, counseling, or healing. She lived humbly, and rejected any more money than she needed to maintain her simple, unpretentious lifestyle. Most of her clothes were given to her, she was driven here and there by her students, and she shared an apartment with a family who loved her and offered her the space. Hilda cared not for fame or power; integrity was more important to her than notoriety. This saintly woman simply sought to uplift souls and improve the quality of their life. She trusted that God would connect her with the people who could benefit from her teachings, and so it was. Hilda welcomed anyone requesting help and she gave generously of her time and talent. People in physical and psychic distress came to her home daily, where she ushered them to her healing room and gave them her compassionate attention. She used her spiritual gifts solely for service and illumination. What a rare soul to walk the earth!

Stage 4 of Spiritual Evolution

You develop relationships with nonphysical guides. The idea that there are illuminated entities beyond your physical sight becomes real and attractive. Open now to higher communication, you encounter invisible beings channeled by other persons, or you connect internally with spiritual masters who present you with more subtle teachings and higher truth.

Don't Sit on the Saint

The first time I went to visit Hilda in her Manhattan apartment, I noticed a row of wooden chairs set against a wall. When I went to sit on one, Hilda told me, "Please don't sit there. Ammal is sitting there."

Ammal was a short, frail, gray-haired Indian woman Hilda knew in Sri Lanka. Hilda described her as a little-known saint who had terrific healing power and performed miracles. After Ammal had passed on, Hilda suggested that we call upon Ammal to help us when necessary. Many students reported healings and miracles as a result of Ammal's intervention. Hilda had invited a number of her invisible friends, including Ammal, to hang out in her apartment, with several chairs reserved for them. I certainly did not want to squash or displace Ammal, so I rose quickly!

Several months later I brought my friend Christine, a gifted clairvoyant, to visit Hilda. Christine had never heard of Ammal and she knew nothing about her. When we entered Hilda's apartment, Christine scanned the empty chairs against the wall and asked me, "Who's the little old lady with gray hair sitting in that chair?"

Finding Common Ground

One of Hilda's most compelling teachings was her unconditional acceptance of all spiritual paths. Her lessons and guidance embraced Christianity, Judaism, Islam, Buddhism, Hinduism, and non-religious penchants. She welcomed agnostics, atheists, and skeptics to her classes. Her unconditional love was greater than any doubt or division. She simply wanted to help people who were suffering and make a positive difference in a world gone weird.

Hilda told us, "A mystic meets on a point of agreement." She demonstrated this by always finding common ground with students and visitors. One night after class I observed a line of students waiting to speak to Hilda. The first person in line wore a pendant bearing the photo of Meher Baba, a beloved Indian mystic. Hilda touched the pendant and with a heartfelt smile remarked, "I love Meher Baba. I met him while I was in India." The next person in line wore a white robe of the Jain tradition. "I had one of my most powerful meditations in a Jain temple," she remarked. Then a woman wearing a gold cross on a necklace approached. "Jesus is the great healer," she noted. And on and on. Everyone felt like Hilda was "one of us." And she was.

Seeing Stars

At the end of each of Hilda's classes, students would line up for healing and blessings. During one period of several months, she would direct energy to students until they were "slain in the spirit" (similar to the practice done in charismatic Christian churches, where a minister touches a congregant seeking help, and that person falls to the floor). Hilda was not affiliated with any particular church or denomination, but she wanted students to experience the many dimensions of healing.

On the eve of my departure on a citizen diplomacy mission to the Soviet Union, I got in line to ask Hilda for a blessing on my journey. Hearing that, she pulled her arm back like a baseball pitcher winding up, and then thrust her palm toward me. To be honest, I was skeptical about the "slain in the spirit" gig and did not expect anything dramatic to happen to me.

Was I wrong! As Hilda thrust her arm in my direction, I saw a surge of energy shooting from it. It reminded me of the old *Batman* TV shows where Batman would punch a villain and a huge cartoon-like star would shoot out of his hand accompanied by huge bold letters like "POW!" The force was irresistible, and I immediately blanked out. The next thing I knew, I was lying on the floor looking up at several assistants who had caught me and gently laid me down. I took a minute to get my bearings, and then rose. When I later visited the Soviet Union, the mission was a huge success.

This teacher's tool kit was bottomless.

Get Real

During a class with a smaller group of advanced students, Hilda asked, "Does anyone here not believe that the ascended masters are real?"

One fellow, Matt, had the courage to raise his hand.

Hilda looked at Matt piercingly and stated bluntly, "They are more real than you are."

While the statement may sound like a jab, it was a profound teaching. Hilda was explaining that we have been hypnotized to believe that we are limited to our physical bodies, personalities, social roles, and the shallow traits that most people identify with. Yet those beings who dwell exclusively in spirit live closer to reality than most of us who are engrossed in the world the physical senses show us. Meanwhile, our spiritual self is our true reality. We might append Hilda's statement to her student to: "The masters are more real than who you think you are."

The ascended masters were Hilda's friends, peers, and partners, closer to her than people who showed up before her in physical bodies. She enjoyed genuine, intimate, lively relationships with nonphysical beings and conversed with them as naturally as you and I might share a worldly conversation. I would go so far as to say that Hilda herself was an ascended master who visited the Earth for a lifetime of service. In all of my spiritual journeys I have never known anyone exactly like her. She transcended all labels. She belonged to all traditions and no tradition. She was in the world but not of it. She carved her own unique spiritual path and encouraged her students to carve theirs. She wanted nothing from the world but to bring it closer to heaven, which she most gracefully achieved.

The word "university" usually applies to institutions of human learning. Yet, after studying with Hilda Charlton and her nonphysical friends, I realize that earthly universities fall short of the true meaning of the word. A real university embraces *all* dimensions of the universe, not simply the world prescribed by the physical senses and intellect. When you study in the university beyond time, the curriculum is endless.

To learn more about the life and teachings of Hilda Charlton, visit www.hildacharlton.com, a website created by Hilda's students after her passing in 1988.

DIRECT CONNECT 12
Meeting the Master

Do you sense that you have a relationship with any particular spirit guide(s)?

If so, do you know your guide(s) by name? If you do, please note:

Can you identify the unique energy, character, or spiritual gifts each guide brings to you?

If so, record below:

Name of Guide   Energy, Traits, or Gifts This Guide Brings Me

What can you do to deepen and solidify your relationship with your guide(s)?

If you have not already done so, establish a conversation with your guide(s). Talk to them as real friends who walk by your side, celebrate your joys, and support you during times of hardship. Turn to them as you need to, and notice how your relationship grows.

✦ ✦ ✦

Affirm:

I am open to know and communicate with my guides in spirit. I welcome your help to advance my life and empower me to serve others. I accept only true guides, masters of light, sent by God. I am blessed to receive and act on help from friends in high places.

WHEN GOD WALKS THE EARTH

While Hilda Charlton was adept at soaring in astral dimensions, she was also meticulous about handling the details of daily life. She was a master at integrating the etheric and the earthly. Many individuals who are enamored with the heavens do not skillfully manage worldly matters and relationships. They tend to space out and make missteps. Not Hilda. To her, spirituality was utterly practical. She kept her head in the clouds and her feet on the ground.

Hilda oversaw a pizza shop run by her students in upper Manhattan, reverently named after the saint Ammal. The eatery was a not-for-profit venture, the income donated to an orphanage in India. Students took turns volunteering as staff. After our celestial classes at St. John the Divine, throngs found their way to Ammal's Pizza to snack and socialize. You can imagine my shock when the first time I entered the shop, there was Hilda wiping down the counter.

My mentor often quoted Jesus, "He who humbles himself shall be exalted," and "Those who would be great must serve." One evening Hilda had invited a guest speaker to address our class in a Manhattan loft. At the conclusion of her presentation, the speaker asked, "Can someone please direct me toward the restroom?" Before any student responded, Hilda spritely rose from her chair at the front of the room and guided the guest to the restroom.

My teacher offered endless tips for staying focused on spiritual purpose in the midst of daily life. For example:

Be a hundred-percenter, not a ninety-nine-percenter. After you wash the dishes, don't leave any scraps of food in the little basket that traps food from going down the drain. Complete the job.

Don't siphon off your energy with nervous habits. For example, don't doodle while on the phone. Be fully present and don't distract yourself if you are bored or uncomfortable. Show up and communicate directly. Make the interaction sufficiently meaningful so you don't have to escape from it.

Don't "one-up" when someone tells a story. Rather than telling your story in response, to equal or better theirs, let the other person receive the validation and acknowledgement for their sharing.

Give anonymously. A certain student used to go to Hilda's apartment and voluntarily clean it when she went out. To let her know that it was he who performed this meritorious act, he regularly left a rose. While Hilda appreciated his work, she explained that his service would have been purer if he did not need to leave a sign drawing attention to himself.

Don't boss your gift. If you give someone a gift, don't be attached to what the recipient does with it. If they never use it, or give it to someone else, that's not your business. The blessing is in the giving. If you attempt to control what happens after you give, what you gave is not a gift.

These are but a few of the many seemingly small but powerful practical tips Hilda imparted. Living them, she explained, carves the difference between a banal existence and a masterful life.

True to Her Values

One winter night Hilda sat on stage wearing an elegant blue sari as she taught her class of over 300 students in the massive legendary cathedral. You can imagine my shock when she lifted the hem of the garment to reveal she was wearing a pair of almost-knee-high red velour go-go boots! "Someone gave me these boots," she explained. "It's a really cold night and they are the warmest shoes I have. I know they don't match my sari, but I didn't want to sit here being cold. I'm more interested in well-being than fashion."

Hilda did not own a car, so no one saw her drive. Then one student had the rare opportunity to see Hilda drive a friend's car with a manual stick shift. The student reported, "I have never seen anyone shift gears so seamlessly and gracefully. I felt no jarring or slippage when the car moved from one gear to the next, like butter. It was as if Hilda was one with the vehicle."

One day a student came to Hilda's apartment building and gave the doorman an envelope for Hilda. It contained $5,000 in cash as a gift. When Hilda examined the contents and heard who the donor was, she decided to return it, since in this case the donation came with sullied motivations. Hilda trusted God as her guide to all events and choices. As a result, she was always cared for, and miracles and blessings continually unfolded around her. "Surely goodness and mercy shall fallow me all the days of my life, and I will dwell in the house of the Lord forever."

Showtime

Coming from a background in dance, Hilda had a penchant for show business. She encouraged students to sing and dance on stage at her classes, and she occasionally organized pageants in which students belted out show tunes and presented skits.

One night I brought my guitar to class and I became one of the regular singers in the small band that entertained at the meetings. Hilda occasionally asked me to solo, a real honor. The honor turned to malaise, however, when she would call on me to play in situations outside the class. Our group purchased a property in upstate New York where we did organic farming and met for summer classes. On some evenings Hilda called out, "Cohen, get your guitar." All of the students piled in cars and jaunted to the local Dairy Queen shop. There I was instructed to sit on an outside bench and play, "All You Need is Love," with everyone in our group singing along. At first, I hated that command public performance, but after several go-rounds I began to enjoy it. Looking back, I realize that while part of Hilda's intention was to lighten the world, another motivation was to get me out of my ego by doing something out of my comfort zone.

One day our farming group took an excursion with Hilda to the famed Howe Caverns, where we took a boat trip with tourists through a huge network of underground caves. There Hilda ordered a trio of her best female singers to pound out a rousing version of "Boogie-Woogie Bugle Boy" in three-part harmony, reverberating off the walls of the cave like a huge concert hall.

We never knew why Hilda asked us to do certain odd acts. But there was always some point to her teachings. She was constantly trying to lighten a burdened world. Mystics are enigmatic and unpredictable. From a worldly point of view, one may puzzle at their motivation, but they always harbor deeper intentions. Hilda introduced us to a yogi in India, Ram Surat Kumar, who regularly served tea to visitors. While chatting afterward, he would seemingly casually arrange the cups and saucers in a precise order. One day when one of the visitors moved a cup, the yogi admonished him, "Please don't touch the teacups. You will ruin my work!"

Hilda explained that the yogi was doing serious prayer and intention work by setting the cups where they were. On a cosmic level, he was setting the world in order. In this case, it was not "tea for two," but order for humanity.

Where Humanity Meets Divinity

I realize that the picture I have offered of Hilda Charlton resembles that of a saint. Truth be told, she was as close to sainthood as anyone I have ever known. Her dedication to integrity and walking the talk was impeccable. She did have her human side as well. Occasionally she would voice her disappointments and frustrations, and she sometimes misread certain individuals or predicted events that did not occur. We got to know Hilda the human being as well as Hilda the friend of the gods. There was equally valuable teaching in those less glorious moments, as they gave us permission to accept our own humanity. Let us not deny valuable spiritual teachings because the teacher occasionally stumbles. Their stumbling is less important than what they make of it. The best teachers use their errors to learn and grow, and pass their triumphs along to their students.

We achieve freedom not by running from life, but by mastering it. Those who believe the world has power over them have not gained spiritual maturity. It is tempting to retreat to an ashram or secluded nature site to gain respite from the pressures and stresses of life. Indeed, retreats have their value. Yet mastering life from within the thick of worldly activity yields magnificent mastery. Those who make daily life work on their behalf, and the behalf of all, graduate with honors.

DIRECT CONNECT 13

Connecting Heaven and Earth

If you have studied with a spiritual teacher, or are studying now:

Is this person grounded as well as spiritual?

Does this person masterfully handle the mundane details of worldly life, or do they tend to be scattered, spaced out, or less than diligent?

Do you masterfully handle the details of your worldly life, or do you tend to be scattered, spaced out, or less than diligent?

Do you know any people who are spiritually aware and simultaneously grounded and efficient? If so, who are they and what have you learned from them?

How can you more masterfully integrate your spiritual life with your worldly life?

STAND AND DELIVER

One night after class I approached Hilda to ask her a question. After she answered, she paused for a moment and studied my face. "How long have you been with me, kid?" (Hilda called everyone "kid," even students 90 years of age.)

"About three years," I replied, puzzled.

"You've taken in long enough. It's time to give out."

"What do you mean?"

"Start teaching. Set up a little group. Find people who need help and give it to them."

I hadn't thought about that. Yet I knew that the master does not utter idle words, so I took Hilda's advice seriously. The following week I placed a small ad in the local newspaper, inviting people to a spiritual study group in my home. We would meet every Sunday evening at no charge. I did not set myself up as a teacher, but rather a facilitator for people who wanted to connect, learn, support each other, and grow.

A handful of people showed up for the first meeting. We enjoyed a stimulating discussion and connecting with seekers of like mind. Over the following weeks, participants took turns sharing various spiritual paths and techniques. One fellow led Native American drumming and chanting. A Reiki practitioner gave a hands-on demonstration of energy healing. A chef showed us how to make tofu. The group grew, and I gained skills in group facilitation. Our format was humble, our interaction meaningful.

Over time, the group evolved into a community potluck dinner, followed by presentations and lively conversation. Word got around, and before long the house was bursting with more people than it could hold. We were fulfilling a need. The weekly event became a local legend and went on for years. After I moved from that city, the gathering continued, hosted by different people at their homes. The group had a life of its own, delivering healing and transformation to the community. It all started with one comment from a dedicated teacher: "It's time to start giving."

Step Forth

Many people tell me they would like to express their gifts as a teacher, psychic, medium, channeler, or healer. Some would like to do this simply as a service, and others would like to work professionally.

I always encourage people to act on their vision, for three good reasons: (1) Many people in the world are struggling or suffering, seeking peace and healing; anyone who offers information or inspiration to make others' lives better is making a huge contribution to humanity. (2) When you teach, you deepen and edify your knowledge of the material you are sharing. You learn what you are teaching. (3) When you are in service, your own problems lighten or dissolve. Many of the holistic life coaches I train report that while they may otherwise be wrapped up in the issues of their life, when they coach they feel liberated and find healing for themselves.

If you fear or resist putting your gifts out there, the ego will make up all kinds of excuses to thwart or delay your progress. *"You are not ready. You have too many issues of your own. You are not worthy. If people knew the truth about you, they would not come to you, let alone pay you. You will look foolish. Your family or friends will laugh at you, criticize, or reject you. You have a secure job; even if you don't like it, it puts food on the table; don't risk your income for a career whose reward is questionable."* And on and on and on.

When you are about to move ahead to do something new, exciting, and spiritually expansive, an old limiting identity is prone to rear up and threaten you, citing all the reasons you shouldn't change your life. Such resistance is a good sign, as it indicates that you are about to step out of a small world inscribed by a false circle of fear, into a new and broader domain. If you do not heed the fearful threats and just keep moving ahead, that dark diminutive voice will eventually give up and you will become established on higher ground.

That small study group I initiated led to a lifetime career of the deepest reward. After a few years, I began to write books and teach workshops that have yielded me soul-fulfilling relationships with many thousands of people, and journeys around the world that have changed my life. Little did I know when Hilda said, "It's time to start giving out," that while I would be giving out to others, the universe would be giving out to me and bestowing soul fulfillment beyond anything I could imagine at the time.

Trust is the Key

If you have a desire or vision to deliver healing, your Higher Power is supporting you at every step. You don't have to know the details about how your teaching or path of service will come about. Simply start, and make use of whatever information or resources you have. Your next steps will be revealed to you in the perfect way and timing. It is said, "When you take one step toward God, God takes ten steps toward you."

If you are worried about what could go wrong, shift your focus to what could go right. The benefits of teaching far outweigh any dangers. You could help many, many people, and potentially earn an income doing what you love. Most important, you will find peace for your soul that hiding in the shadows could never deliver.

Just as "when the student is ready, the teacher appears," when the teacher is ready, the students appear. Even if you are not a formal teacher, you constantly teach by your being. Every action demonstrates faith or its absence. When you are aligned with universal truth, you uplift everyone you meet. The plan for connecting teachers and students who belong to each other runs far deeper than the human mind can fathom. Blessed are you for being so loved that Great Spirit sends you precisely who you can help relieve their suffering, and in turn lift your own life into the light.

DIRECT CONNECT 14
Stand and Deliver

Would you like to teach what you have learned or are learning?

If so, what would you like to offer?

Do you believe you are ready to teach?

If not, why not?

What does the voice of fear or unworthiness say about you stepping forth to teach?

What does the voice of courage, confidence, or joy say?

If you were to move ahead as a teacher, what would be the next step to make that happen?

How could you benefit spiritually and/or materially by teaching what you are passionate about?

How could others benefit from your service, and the world become a better place?

PART IV

HELEN:

THE RELUCTANT MIRACLE WORKER

PLEASE TAKE NOTES

If a mysterious voice told you to take dictation for a message to humanity that could save the world, would you do it? If the content was completely foreign to your beliefs, would you trust it? And if you resisted intensely, but the voice persisted, would you surrender? That is precisely the predicament in which Dr. Helen Schucman found herself. How she responded has profoundly transformed the lives of millions.

Dr. Schucman, although Jewish by culture, an atheist by philosophy, and a conservative psychologist by profession, had had a number of precognitive dreams, visions, and psychic perceptions during her lifetime. As professor of medical psychology at Columbia University's College of Physicians and Surgeons, she was immersed in a milieu of ongoing argument, competition, and backbiting, as is often the case in academia. She was getting along especially poorly with her supervisor, Dr. Bill Thetford. After an extended period of acrimony, Bill came to Helen and suggested, "There must be a better way." Helen agreed, and the two set out on the journey to heal and rebuild their relationship.

Four months later, Dr. Schucman heard a voice say, "This is a course in miracles. Please take notes." The voice identified itself as Jesus Christ. Since Helen regularly counseled people who heard voices—that of Jesus raising an especially red flag—she was quite hesitant to heed this one, let alone talk about it. But when the voice persisted, she confided in Dr. Thetford. "Bill, I'm hearing a voice telling me to take notes for a course in miracles. . .What do you think I should do?" Dr. Thetford thought for a moment and responded, "Maybe you should take notes."

Sequestered in her Manhattan apartment, Helen grabbed a shorthand notebook and recorded the words she was hearing. The next morning she brought her notepad to the office, where she sheepishly read it to Bill, coughing and practically choking to get the words out. To Helen's surprise, Bill was impressed and inspired by the material. He wanted to see more and, to Helen's dismay, encouraged her to continue. He agreed to work with her to bring the material forth. Bill was a skilled typist, so Helen agreed to take dictation at home and Bill agreed to type it as Helen later transmitted it to him via spoken word.

Every weekday morning and some Saturdays, the two locked themselves in Bill's office, pulled down the shades, and transferred the messages onto paper. This process went on for seven years, until three volumes had come: a Text, a Workbook for Students, and a Manual for Teachers, totaling 1127 printed pages.

The content of *A Course in Miracles* revealed:

- We are all spiritual beings by nature.
- God is present in us and around us.
- Love is the only reality.
- Our purpose is to be happy.
- Every thought, feeling, and action represents a choice between fear and love.

- Fear, sorrow, suffering, and sacrifice are never required or justified.
- There is no sin; guilt is purposeless.
- We struggle because we believe in the illusion of separation.
- The way to healing and inner peace is through forgiveness.
- A happy outcome to all things is sure.
- There is no death.

The Course's definition of forgiveness goes far beyond what most people understand as forgiveness, which is to overlook or not seek revenge for an injury that someone else has perpetrated. Instead, the Course suggests that no one has the power to hurt you unless you see yourself as limited and powerless. When you shift your perception to recognize that you are eternally whole, loved, innocent, and not subject to adverse external forces, you become invulnerable to worldly events, and you experience inner peace as your divine inheritance.

While I could write endlessly about the principles and healing power of *A Course in Miracles**, my intention here is not so much to explain the content, but to illuminate the process by which it came, what the channeler experienced, and—most importantly—how you can use these extraordinary dynamics to enhance the quality of your life.

There are forces of love and wisdom that call human beings to deliver important messages of guidance and upliftment to the world. Channeling and healing are co-creations of people and invisible sources. If you feel called to "take dictation," as Helen Schucman did, trust that your inspiration

---

* For an in-depth exploration and application of *A Course in Miracles*, see my book and/or online course *A Course in Miracles Made Easy: Mastering the Journey from Fear to Love*.

is coming from a valid source, which will benefit you by recording it, and humanity for receiving it. When you act on your guidance, even if you have fear, hesitation, or resistance, it becomes real in the world for you and everyone you influence.

DIRECT CONNECT 15
Please Take Notes

Take pen and paper, your computer or mobile device, and sit quietly in prayer or meditation for a few minutes. When your mind becomes still and you feel receptive, ask your inner guidance, "What would you have me know to come to greater peace and make my life better?"

Record the guidance you have received.

Then, "What would you have me know that would enhance my contribution to humanity, beginning with the people close to me?

Record this guidance now.

Sit with the information you received and absorb it into the depths of your being. Then get on with your day, trusting that all the opportunities to put your guidance into practice will be shown to you. If you received guidance to take a specific action, move in that direction and observe the results.

A DEEPER AGREEMENT

The stark contrast between the intense urging of the *Course in Miracles* material and Helen Schucman's resistance to it, and the misfit of her belief system with the philosophy of the Course, provides the most compelling illustration of the reality of a soul contract between the source and the channel. As I have noted, the interaction between a channel and the guiding entity is the result of an agreement the two made before the channel's birth, far deeper than the channel's personality. Helen and Jesus mutually consented that at a crucial point in her life he would contact her and ask her to deliver the material to the world. When the time was ripe, that agreement was fulfilled.

As in many channeling relationships, the channel's lifestyle, history, training, philosophy, and religious or spiritual beliefs are not essential to this contract. Those attributes dwell at the surface level of ego, body, personality, and cultural conditioning. Soul agreements run far deeper. Some channels are already on the spiritual path, dabbling in or studying meditation, prayer, healing, or some esoteric practice. Others are quite distant from a spiritual path, immersed in worldly activities and lifestyles quite foreign to expanded awareness. Yet the soul's choices supersede the channel's personal history or the whims of their ego or personality.

Even odder, while Helen eventually surrendered to the process of channeling, or "scribing," as she called it, and the material flowed smoothly without resistance on her part, she never really adopted the values of the Course or practiced it as students are asked. She accepted her role to bring *A Course in Miracles* to the world, but not to her life. This curious predicament was quite stressful for this extraordinary woman whose service to humanity was paramount. Helen once offered an enigmatic yet telling statement about her relationship with the Course: "I know it's true, but I don't believe it." In other words, her spirit recognized the Course's reality and value, while her personality rejected it.

That statement is particularly apt when we recognize the mixed bag of themes that coursed through Helen Schucman's life. On one hand she was a rational, cynical, strong-willed, stubborn scientist, self-described as a "militant atheist." On the other hand she was deeply connected with vaster realms, tapped into dimensions far beyond the Earth, and she sincerely wanted to help. She experienced intense visionary dreams and psychic impressions. She also had a devotional heart, poetically revealed through the book she wrote independent of the channeled Course, entitled *The Gifts of God.*

Helen's dualistic nature and puzzling relationship to Spirit serves as a powerful teaching for us all. We all experience a split mind. We are all connected to God and we simultaneously kick and scream when we are invited to own and express our divinity. We run shallow and we run deep. Helen Schucman's dramatic internal schism between faith and doubt represents the tightrope we all walk. We can be grateful to this rare soul for more than just delivering *A Course in Miracles.* We can thank her for highlighting the humanness we all face, and motivating us to integrate it with the spiritual gifts that come to us and through us.

DIRECT CONNECT 16
Soul Contracts

We all have soul contracts with the people in our lives who have most profoundly influenced our journey. When we understand that those who love us, as well as those who challenge us, come to us by divine agreement for our soul's growth, we can appreciate and bless all of our relationships.

Identify one person with whom you have a soul contract in which that person loves, supports, and empowers you:

How has this person helped you to advance on your spiritual path?

Identify one person with whom you have a soul contract in which that person challenges you:

How have you learned and grown through your relationship with that person?

Identify one person with whom you have a soul contract for that person to support you and also challenge you:

How have you learned and grown through both their support and their challenge?

Do you believe you have a spirit guide or guardian angel who has guided and protected you throughout your life, and/or delivered inspiration or information for you to share with the world?

If so, what do you believe is the nature of your soul contract with that higher entity?

What does your guide want you to know about where you now stand on your spiritual path, and what your next step(s) might be?

Permission to Edit

Although some early Course historians indicated that *A Course in Miracles* came word for word and Helen simply took notes as she heard the teachings, a great deal of after-the-fact editing took place as a co-creation between Jesus and Helen. If you study the stenographic pads on which Helen wrote (available to view online), you will see that a significant portion of the material, mostly at the beginning of the Text, was changed, Jesus guiding Helen to delete here, add here, substitute there. Helen attributed this process to her imperfect recording of the material, and the shared intent of both Jesus and Helen to bring forth the most accurate expression of its meaning.

When I learned about this process, I felt relieved and empowered. When I write, I never use the first draft. I get the basic ideas onto paper, and then go over each page many times, cutting and pasting until the content says exactly what I want it to say. Knowing that a document as profound as *A Course in Miracles*, sourced by no less than Jesus Christ, also went through a revision process, gave me permission to not have to be perfect at anything on the first attempt. Perhaps knowing this will relieve you, too, of any notion that the first pass has to be the final cut.

I also found it comforting that Jesus was willing to work patiently with Helen until the material was molded into its proper form. We are co-creators with God. In a sense, God needs us as much as we need God. When we are aligned with the divine, we serve as God's voice in the world. *A Course in Miracles* Workbook Lesson 353 calls us to avow, "My eyes, my tongue, my hands, my feet today have but one purpose; to be given Christ to use to bless the world with miracles."

The Recording Secretary

A Course in Miracles came to Helen Schucman in a continuous stream, in spite of interruptions by the activities required by her daily life. She would be taking the Course's dictation, for example, when the doorbell would ring and she would attend to the visitor. When that interaction was complete, she would return to her scribing and pick it up from the word she had left off, to complete the sentence in a coherent and meaningful way. She also took dictation while riding in taxicabs and on the subway.

This method confirms a dynamic I have experienced in writing, which you might recognize in your own creative process. I believe that a book or any other creative work is already written in the ethers, or the mind of God, or the Akashic Record, or whatever divine source you recognize. My job as an author, or yours as a painter, musician, producer, teacher, parent, or entrepreneur, is to tap into the material that already exists and bring it to earth in a form true to the source. Thus we might say that geniuses are more like secretaries than inventors. They take dictation purely and replicate heavenly works on earth. Master scientist Nikola Tesla reported that the ideas for his inventions came to him in a flash of inspired insight. Then he worked them out in his mind. By the time he reached the laboratory, the plans were complete, and all he had to do was match the material expression with the vision. The role of secretary or lab assistant does not demean a genius, but honors him or her as being a clear window through which a greater light can shine.

Each of us is appointed a role to bring heaven to earth in a unique way that matches our vision, passion, and talents. If you do not believe you are worthy, or you doubt your source, or you fear exposing yourself to criticism, the material will have a harder time getting through. You could even block it entirely. Yet you can also allow it entirely. Practice trusting that your inspiration is coming from a mighty benevolent source, and fulfill your agreement to be a channel of blessings and healing.

Dr. Helen Schucman was a human being who served nobly to deliver a divine gift to the world. In spite of her fears and resistance, she fulfilled that role impeccably. *A Course in Miracles* has uplifted the lives of millions of people, and brought them healing and hope. You and I share the capacity to deliver our own gifts. Let us accept our function humbly, and claim our role as servants of truth that ripples out to touch, bless, and heal more people than we can imagine.

DIRECT CONNECT 17
Deliver Your Gift

What message, gift, or service do you believe Higher Power wants you to deliver to humanity?

What signs or confirmations have you received that demonstrate that this is your soul's true path?

What fears or resistance do you have to delivering your gifts?

What is the best thing that could happen if you found the courage to act on your guidance?

What would be your next step to share your gifts with the world?

PART V

EMMANUEL:

ENJOY THE RIDE

A MANUAL OF LOVE

Pat Rodegast was just minding her own business when he showed up. He was not the man of her dreams, but he helped her awaken from her dreams. His name was Emmanuel, and he had no body. But he was beautiful beyond words.

This vibrant yet humble woman had been working as a secretary for a publishing company, while raising three teenagers. To quiet her mind, she began to practice Transcendental Meditation. Soon she began to experience visions. Eventually the images expanded into a bright light accompanied by a voice. As Pat became more familiar and comfortable with this presence, he introduced himself as a spirit guide named "Emmanuel."

Over time, Pat became a clear channel for this gentle poetic spirit. She began to do private readings for clients who were deeply impressed by Emmanuel's loving presence and wise guidance. Eventually word about Emmanuel got to Ram Dass, one of the most respected leaders of the emerging spiritual movement in the world.

When Ram Dass introduced Emmanuel to the public through his lectures, he offered this witty description:

Many people are very sensitive to prejudice these days. We seek to rise above it and embrace all people. Most prejudice has to do with bodies and their appearances. We judge by gender, race, age, weight, disability, cultural, and religious customs. But there is still one form of prejudice we have yet to address and overcome: prejudice against having no body. You tell people, "I speak to a spirit without a body," and they say, "That's not real. You're nuts." Perhaps prejudice against having no body is the final frontier of prejudice we need to overcome. There are lots of people without bodies we must respect because we can learn a great deal from them.

Ram Dass later extolled Emmanuel as a source of wisdom:

I have had the opportunity to get to know Emmanuel's teachings and as a psychologist I have realized that it does not matter how Pat is able to communicate these teachings because the truth and intuitive validity of what Emmanuel says is what really matters. He has a certain charm, warmth and humor that has made me treasure him as a friend. So, whether that information is coming from the deepest part of Pat or from another being or from the highest one that lies beyond all forms, it does not matter as long as it helps guide us home.

Teachings from the Heart

I met Pat and Emmanuel when we were simultaneously presenting classes at a retreat sponsored by Omega Institute on the island of St. John in the Caribbean. I immediately felt at ease in Pat's presence. She had no airs or ego about her role as a channel; her sincere intention to heal spoke from the core of her being. Pat never sought fame or power, she was not enmeshed in an organization, and money was not her motivator. When I met Pat, she was in her sixties, attractive and vivacious as a woman much younger. When she reached her late seventies, Pat's doctor told her that all of her vital signs matched those of a woman in her early fifties. If channeling youthens a person by twenty-five years, sign me up!

Pat was a partial-trance channel. She clearly heard Emmanuel's voice while she was channeling, and regarded herself as an audience along with those who listened. While channeling, she would occasionally comment on a phrase that Emmanuel had just spoken, adding, "Wow, I never thought of it like that," or, "That's so beautiful!" or she let forth a soft giggle. This channel was simply passing along what she heard.

Emmanuel is another name for Jesus. It means "God is with us." Sitting with Emmanuel was, I am certain, like sitting with Jesus himself. His teachings are simple, innocent, and lyrical, and they speak to the soul. No complexity, abstractions, mystical esoteric language, or a regimen of hoops to jump through. *God is here and you are loved. All else is detail.* This spiritual master reduces all answers to the language of the heart. Zero judgment, dogma, rituals, or prerequisites for awakening. Even while Emmanuel's teachings are majestic, a conversation with him was as relaxed as sharing tea with a dear friend. He spoke with no accent, affectation, or drama. When I sat with Emmanuel, I felt immersed in a warm bath of soothing compassion.

One of Emmanuel's unique gifts was telling "bedtime stories," soft fables that illustrated humanity's journey into density and then our return to love. He invited students at retreats to stretch out on the floor and become children again, this time for stories that led them out of illusion rather than deeper into it.

I was fortunate to spend a fair amount of time with Pat and Emmanuel, and I regard both of them as supremely dear friends and guides. I learned as much from the way they carried themselves, as I did from their words. If kindness, humility, and gentleness are attributes of God's teachers, then Emmanuel and Pat were very close to God, and they called us to meet them there.

Here are some of my favorite gems from Emmanuel. They illustrate how lofty truth can be captured in a sentence or two:

What you love to do the most is the shortest distance between where you are now and your dreams.

You are not a beggar at the table of life. You are the honored guest.

The challenge is to believe your dreams in the center of illusion.

Fear tells you to fulfill the expected. Love says, "May I have this dance?"

You are 100% safe all the time.

All love returns to you. All fear returns to dust.

Remove the lens fear has taught you to wear.

Don't be impatient with yourself. Just be in awe.

Love called you here. Love will see you through.

Where Is Everybody?

One evening at the St. John retreat, Pat and Emmanuel presented a program in an open-air pavilion high atop a hill with a stunning sunset view. The panorama was breathtaking: a majestic gold, amber, and purple sunset; several Caribbean islands visible in the distance; the tranquil harbor dotted with sailboats, pelicans gracefully soaring on thermals. The scene was a picture postcard in three dimensions, as close to heaven as Earth comes. The quiet embrace of that image is forever etched in my mind.

When I arrived at the large gazebo, Pat was sitting in a chair ready to channel, her back to the sunset—a sight to soothe the weariest soul. I pulled up a cushion on the floor close to Pat and readied myself for an evening in the presence of pure love. As I turned to scan the audience, I was surprised to find only a handful of people. I could not understand why all the other conference participants were absent. I imagine they were going out to dinner on their vacation time. But from my perspective, nothing that lovely island had to offer was more valuable than sitting in the presence of Christ himself. Who would choose red snapper over the Sermon on the Mount? Yet I wasn't complaining. I was blessed with a practically private session in which I asked lots of questions and received meaningful personal feedback.

I did glean some valuable lessons from the experience:

1. Not everyone is ready to hear the voice of liberation. We are masters of distraction, finding endless ways to avoid the light. *A Course in Miracles* tells us that pure love calls forth everything unlike itself. If you are holding any fear, judgment, or resistance when faced with genuine love, that resistance will amplify, and you will leave the room mentally or physically.

113

2. Not every teaching is for everyone. Emmanuel spoke directly to my soul, but other people have other teachers and methods that speak directly to their soul. To believe that my teacher must be everyone's teacher is an expression of ego. The path that works for others is not my business. I can accept, bless, and release others to walk their own path. My role is to discover my unique path and be true to it.

3. All spiritual teachers have their own bent and intentions about their ministry or career. Some channels are attracted to fame, fortune, and moving in the public eye. Others avoid the limelight; they simply teach those who are attracted to them without fanfare or promotion. They prefer to maintain a quality of life free of the media and people wanting lots of things from them. The paths of fame and anonymity each have their pros and cons. Each teacher must choose the path most befitting their choice and destiny.

4. Never evaluate the quality of a spiritual teacher or teaching by the number of people in the audience. Some of most gifted teachers fly under the radar, while some of the most popular teachers are compromised.

Integrity Recognizes Integrity

Pat and Emmanuel were not into show business. Their business was love; all else was an afterthought. Emmanuel did not make predictions, an attention-getter that many psychics parlay. He simply laid out spiritual truth and gave his audiences tools to carve their own destiny.

I used to see Pat at the uplifting "Celebrate Your Life" conferences in Phoenix. At that time the programs were overseen by a lovely woman named Arielle Wolf, who had outlived her cancer diagnosis and wanted to help others maximize their quality of life.

Most of the presenters at the conference were headliners, chosen largely for their high profile and the numbers of people they would draw to the conference. These were bestselling authors who had appeared on *Oprah* or PBS, and had voluminous followings. Their breakout sessions numbered in hundreds of participants. Whenever my schedule allowed, I would sit in on Pat and Emmanuel's session, a breath of fresh air for the soul.

Like the meeting at the St. John event, Pat's crowd was considerably smaller than that of the other better-known presenters, maybe fifty people in the audience. Again, I was amazed. When I left the room after those holy sessions, my heart swelled with respect for conference director Arielle. She wasn't making any money on Pat and Emmanuel. She simply wanted to bring quality teaching to her audience. That was one of the reasons those conferences were so successful. They were guided by heart, not greed. When we place Spirit first, all else follows naturally.

Bring On the Pasta

One of my most delightful memories of being with Pat and Emmanuel was a week-long seminar we co-presented in Assisi, Italy, the home of the beloved St. Francis. Pat loved Assisi as a second home and spent a great deal of time in that charming city. We presented our program each day and then roamed the narrow winding streets of the citadel at night, sampling the best of Assisi's restaurants.

A connoisseur of fine food, Pat guided me to her favorite eateries, where we ate pasta galore. I usually do not eat pasta, but that week I put my diet on hold. It was so much fun to be with Pat and watch her enjoy those lavish meals; I was totally enrolled. Pat was not an ascetic. She enjoyed worldly delights, which gave me a new model of making peace with my body. I tended to be more regimented and kept physical indulgences at a distance, but after hanging out with Pat that week, my resistance dissolved. She lived in harmony with her physical journey. As a result, the food was blessed. I felt good after every meal and I did not gain any weight. I pondered that Pat, who remained eternally trim and fit, would do well to offer seminars for people seeking to lose weight or be content with the diet they enjoyed. In that arena she taught beautifully by example. Pat was simultaneously a channel for a highly evolved spirit, and a human being on her own spiritual journey.

An Elegant Legacy

Pat Rodegast continued her humble yet powerful channeling of Emmanuel until her passing in 2012. Together the two bestowed an elegant legacy. Three books, *Emmanuel's Book I, II,* and *III,* form a substantial written treasury. The website continued by her students, www.spiritofemmanuel. com, as well as YouTube, offer a number of audio and video recordings of sessions with Emmanuel, all material of the highest quality, honoring a rare and noble contribution to humanity.

DIRECT CONNECT 18
The Simplicity of Salvation

Do you complicate your perception of your spiritual path or imagine a gap between where you are and where you think you should be?

If you allowed your spiritual journey and your worldly activities to be simpler and easier, how would you be approaching them differently?

Do you believe that spiritual success is gauged by a number of followers? If so, would you reconsider to use quality of results as a benchmark rather than count of bodies?

If you are a teacher or leader, can you be satisfied with the people that Spirit sends to you without anxiously trying to gather more followers? Can you allow the number of your students to be determined by Great Spirit, and trust that all your needs will be met as you align with Spirit's will?

Are you at peace with your body? Can you enjoy the physical world rather than resisting it?

If you trusted love implicitly, how would you be living differently?

YOUR PAST ISN'T WHAT
IT USED TO BE

Many people have asked Emmanuel about past or future incarnations. I don't recall Emmanuel giving detailed readings about other incarnations. He was more interested in students addressing, healing, and mastering the issues of the current life, and rising to the highest vibration right where we stand.

Being with Emmanuel was like coming home after a long journey. He emphasized the power and importance of living in the present moment. If something from a past life remains an element in your mental or emotional body, it will show up in this life and you will have a golden opportunity to heal it. You don't need to understand or return to where it came from. When you heal the issue now, it completes any lessons inaugurated in a past experience.

The principle is likewise valid for any pattern that occurs within one life. If, for example, you grew up with an oppressive father that resulted in you having an issue with male authority figures, you will tend to attract overbearing men. Each time this occurs, you have a crucial opportunity to master the lesson by claiming your power and worth and recognizing your equality with the person who *seemed* to have power over you. You don't need to go back to your relationship with your father in this life or previous ones. All the healing you need is right where you stand.

Emmanuel spoke of reincarnation in this way:

> Therefore, you, as human personalities,
> see yourselves separated from who you really are.
> It is the clothes you have donned
> in each incarnation
> to impersonate who you are.

Emmanuel is emphasizing that we are souls, not personalities, and the bodies and human characteristics we step into but cloak our true selves. The sincere spiritual aspirant does not get tangled in analyzing physical or emotional issues, but penetrates through them to realize our original spiritual nature.

Is Understanding Reincarnation Useful?

While we often associate reincarnation with eastern religions, the doctrine was an accepted element of Christianity until the Synod of Constantinople in 543 A.D., when the church rejected the philosophy because it gave adherents too much latitude and they could not be pressured to follow the church's dogma in one lifetime. If reincarnation is real, we get many chances to experience life from many different perspectives and learn what we missed the last time around. My mentor Hilda once noted, "If you got here once, you can get here again."

But is the idea of reincarnation useful? Can it make a difference in our daily life on earth, or is it just a speculative distraction? *A Course in Miracles* tells us that the concept of reincarnation can be helpful if it bestows us with a broader picture of life and extends our awareness of our self beyond one life in one body. But, the Course also teaches, the ultimate goal of our human journey is to learn that we are not the body at all. Spirit cannot be born and It cannot die. Our true identity spans far beyond what happens to one or many bodies. The Course does not take a position on reincarnation, because to say it is one way or the other might alienate those who believe otherwise, and the Course would not wish to lose people who could benefit from its teachings. The Course finally suggests that if the idea of reincarnation is helpful to you, then go with it; if not, you are just fine.

Reincarnation Myths and Majesties

Having traveled for many years in circles of people on the spiritual path, I have heard all kinds of ideas and stories about reincarnation. Some are mind-expanding and others are laughable. Some beliefs lead to liberation and others nail human beings in coffins of limits. Let's start with the uplifting, freeing perspectives:

1. My true self exists far beyond the body. *A Course in Miracles* calls us to remember, *I am not a body. I am free. I am still as God created me.* Most—maybe all—of our problems come from identifying with a body. We define ourselves as confined within our skin, and we believe that "what happens to the body happens to me." The pleasures, comfort, and appearance of the body become the consuming theme of life. When undesirable things happen to the body, as minor as getting stuck in a traffic jam, we suffer. Spiritual awakening, on the other hand, reminds us that our real self is not defined by birth, death, time, or what the body is doing. We are not physical, but spiritual; not form, but energy; not the fears associated with mortal experience, but the love associated with rising above it.

Most people who have near-death experiences recount entering a state of ecstatic bliss. For the short time they are free of the body, they are happier than they have ever been in a body. Such glimpses of heaven bestow the recipients with unshakeable certainty in a broader reality. When these people return to physical awareness, they serve as scouts who have peered over the mountain, seen the Promised Land, and returned to tell us what's in store for all of us. They no longer fear death and, buoyed by expanded vision, the quality of their life is elevated.

Such accounts are sometimes misinterpreted to lead us to believe the body is sinful or a curse. Then we judge, resist, torture, or attempt to discard it. Yet we walk the earth for a reason. God does not wish for us to hurt ourselves in any way, and takes no joy in our self-abuse. When we see ourselves as a victim of the body, we project undue power onto it. The body is neutral, no more good or evil than the car you drive. You can use your car to take you to meet someone you love, or you can wreak destruction by driving drunk. The car is not the angel or devil; it is the driver's state of mind that determines its value and results. The body becomes our friend when we make peace with it and use it to discover, celebrate, and communicate love. Those who know God, even while in a body, become the greatest teachers and healers. Go beyond the body when you can in meditation, prayer, and spiritual practice. When you return, use it as a vehicle to express the divinity within you and acknowledge the spiritual reality of all souls.

2. What I do returns to me. Reincarnation teachings always include the principle of karma, the idea that "what goes around comes around." Everything we do affects ourselves and others. When we act with kindness, we shall be treated lovingly. If we act harshly, we shall be treated cruelly.

Reincarnation is often offered as an explanation for diseases and sorrows that occur in this life as the result of misdeeds in previous lives. Childhood illnesses, bad marriages, and apparent accidents, we are taught, stem from our errors or mistreatment of others in previous incarnations. In this sense, every event serves to balance prior acts and teach us where we have erred, that we may correct our mistakes and reconcile our karmic account.

While such suggestions may or may not be true from life to life, they teach a key principle that can help us in this life. Our actions have effects. We do not live in a vacuum. Not only do our kind or cruel deeds affect others, but they impact ourselves. All of the principles explained by karma over many lives are true within this life. Whether you live one life or many, you are accountable for your actions. If a belief in reincarnation stimulates an individual to be more conscious of the karma he or she is creating, and that individual takes care to upgrade his or her actions, the teaching has served well.

3. My encounters and relationships are not random. Many of the people we meet, especially significant relationships, carry over from previous lives, we are taught. This applies to rewarding connections as well as challenging ones. If you have karma with someone from a past life, the Law of Attraction will put you together in this life to complete what you started.

Whether or not this is true for many lives, it is true within one life. If you have a person in your life who is important to your spiritual growth, you will keep meeting that person or their energetic equal.

After college I backpacked in Europe with a friend for the summer. During my first week in England, I met a girl who worked at the American Express office and we had a brief but tumultuous romance that left me with hard feelings. I went on through Europe carrying pain and judgments about her. Over ten weeks' travel I had many adventures that matured me and helped me release my upset. On my last day of the trip I had to go to the American Express office in Amsterdam. To my shock, the same girl was working behind the counter. By that time, I had gotten over my hurt and we had a pleasant interaction. I had graduated from the lesson she came to help me learn, and our relationship was healed and complete.

Even if you do not re-meet an individual with whom you have karma from a past life or this one, you will meet other people who embody the same traits or energy. Countless coaching clients have told me that they keep attracting alcoholics, or fall in love with people who are unavailable, or keep "marrying my father." While such patterns may seem an inescapable curse, they are really a blessing. Repetitive relationships offer valuable lessons calling you to recognize the teaching. You may need to learn to honor yourself by setting healthy boundaries; or quit trying to rescue people from situations they need to resolve for themselves; or rise above your fears and judgments about the opposite sex; or let down your guard and open your heart to someone worthy of your love. If you have gotten out of balance, your karmic relationships offer you an opportunity to restore that balance. If you have wandered into illusions, karma helps you dissolve those illusions by applying a higher truth. Whether you keep breaking up with the same person and getting back together with him, or if you break up and meet someone who replicates him, you have the same golden opportunity for spiritual advancement.

You may also have positive karmic relationships in which you keep meeting kind and loving people who support you; or you attract abundance though whatever job or project you focus on; or you meet spiritual teachers that empower you; or you enjoy a healthy body. None of these situations are random. Everything that shows up in your world is a reflection of your consciousness.

4. I have eternity to find healing and heaven. One damaging belief put forth by some religions is that you have but one life to get it right. If you do, you prance through the pearly gates to enjoy paradise forever. If not, you go to the cosmic hotspot for eternity, consumed by everlasting flames while nasty little devils poke you with pitchforks. If you don't find the one personal savior that everyone on Earth must bow before, you are forsaken by God. Even a little intelligent or compassionate thought reveals how short-sighted, immature, and dogmatic such teachings are.

Every human being has fears, challenges, and karma to deal with. Some have more than others. We are all learning and growing as we go. To demand that you attain liberation and get all of your karma paid off in forty, sixty, or eighty years is an overwhelming and virtually impossible task to ask of anyone. What loving God would send His child to Earth with all of its pressures, dark programming, and insanity, and then consign him to eternal hell for not getting it totally right by the time he exits stage left? People who labor under this psychic whip are unduly burdened. Only a fearful, wrathful, uncompassionate God would set up such a brutal system. No wise soul would ever go there.

The idea that you will go to hell unless you find Jesus Christ, Buddha, Mohammed, or any particular messenger of God, is equally unreasonable and brutish. Not everyone on the planet is going to hear about Jesus Christ, and not everyone needs to. The Christ is a principle more than a person; an experience more than a name. When we reach the mountaintop of truth, names and forms drop away in the blazing presence of eternal, unconditional, compassionate love. Christians who believe they have to proselytize every human being to join their church are shortsighted. They are confusing Jesus with the Christ. Jesus was the man. Christ is a title meaning "the illuminated one." That pure soul was and is the son of God, but, despite what evangelists tell you, he was not the only one. Jesus was the body; Christ is the spirit. Some people, like Jesus, have awakened to their divine identity. They have walked the earth as models of who we will all be when we remember who we are. Ultimately everyone has to find their way home to God, whether you find that way through Christ, Allah, Yahweh, or Mister Rogers. We are all destined to enter heaven, after one life or many.

5. I have a positive alternate identity. If you have poor self-esteem in this life, believing that you were a kind, famous, holy, or wealthy person in a previous life can give your self-image a boost and create positive, practical carryovers right where you stand. Ultimately a divine identity, whether you attribute it to St. Francis, Joan of Arc, Mother Teresa, or any other saintly person, is far closer to the real you than the frail, mortal, limited self you have been programmed to adopt. *A Course in Miracles* urges us to identify only with the noble traits of God, for that is who we truly are.

Previews of Coming Distractions

While a healthy understanding of reincarnation can be empowering, many people use the concept to reinforce limits and deepen suffering. I hear more misuses of reincarnation than I hear uplifting ones. Here are some of them:

1. Feeding ego. I mentioned above that seeing yourself as a successful person in a previous life can be a good ego boost for this life. Yet a healthy ego is not the same a bloated ego. You can hide behind the notion of being a historical celebrity. It's amazing to me how many different people were Cleopatra, St. John of the Cross, William Shakespeare, Abraham Lincoln, and Florence Nightingale. I rarely hear about past lives of people who were goat herders, bartenders, or convicts. If you can't be someone famous in this life, why not be someone famous a century ago? This can be affirming to believe, but past-century accolades become a distraction if you fall back on your historical laurels rather than progressing in your life now.

2. An excuse for not doing your spiritual homework. Believing you were Thomas Jefferson scribing the Declaration of Independence does not absolve you from being kind to your ex-wife or ex–husband now. If you are still here, you have opportunities, lessons, and challenges to face, all of which will advance your spiritual growth. Regardless of what went before, you must handle what is in front of you.

You may also fall prey to blaming your perceived past predicament to justify your current hardship. If you were a peon burdened by oppressive landlords in medieval England, you cannot use that as an excuse to judge people with money now, and thus keep money at a distance from yourself. If your husband in eighteenth century Spain left you for a young wench and you have married him again in this life, you can't justify cheating on him now. If your cough in rural France led to your death during the reign of Louis XVI, don't expect your current cough to kill you, and avoid doing what it takes to get healed in this century.

People who paint themselves as victims in past incarnations cannot afford to continue a victim mentality in this one. The very purpose of becoming aware of that experience might be to help you move beyond that limiting belief and attain mastery of the conditions before you.

3. Reinforcing guilt. You might be tempted to justify a bad situation now as punishment for sins in your past life. If you have a nasty boss in your current job, you might believe you need to stay because you tortured that person in days gone by. People make up all kinds of cockamamie stories to substantiate their suffering and perpetuate unpleasant predicaments. Entire religions have been built around paying off guilt. Any situation in which you accept pain or abuse from someone else represents self-abuse. No one can hurt you unless you agree to be hurt. Your lesson in such situations is to withdraw your agreement that you deserve pain and do what it takes to get free.

4. Manipulation. Some people use the idea of reincarnation as a manipulative tool, for example:

Self-serving and profit. A reader or channeler tells the client that she was a wonderful, talented, or famous person in a previous life, which gives the client an ego rush, justifies the fee she is paying for the reading, and keeps her coming back for more readings.

Entrapment in a cult. Some cults tell their followers that they need the cult to help them pay off their karma. The follower, they suggest, has done dark deeds in previous lives, and the cult can help them cancel out their debt. "Don't dare think about leaving, or you will be sucked back into the dark cycle and never escape." What the cult doesn't tell the follower is that it is a part of the dark cycle.

Sexual or romantic enticement. I was sitting in a hot tub at a retreat with another fellow and a very attractive woman he had met at the retreat. "I have a strong feeling we were together in a previous life," I overheard him tell her. I had to force myself to keep from gagging. Such a manipulation is one station short of offering sexual healing. Fundamentalists say, "The devil quotes scripture." He also quotes reincarnation.

5. Spiritual laziness. People who believe in reincarnation may be tempted to get lazy as they tell themselves, "I have plenty of time to learn and grow. If I don't get it right this time, I will get it right next time." While this may be so, what such people don't realize is that their delay in learning is costing them suffering. When you put off mastering your spiritual lessons, you are putting off your healing. When you put off healing, you stay in pain. *A Course in Miracles* advises, "Delay does not matter in eternity, but it is tragic in time." Don't fall prey to an overwhelming obligation to become perfect in this one life, but also don't unduly tolerate your suffering or anyone's. The Course tells us that the only purpose of time is to learn to use it wisely. Your purpose in life is to get free of illusions and find inner peace as soon as possible, and help others do the same.

The Bigger Picture

While it is fascinating to explore individuals you may have been, in the grandest scheme of things, *you have been and done it all.* As an expression of God reaching into form, you are all of God in all forms. You have been the saint and the sinner; the billionaire and the beggar; the murderer and the victim; Lord Brahma the creator and Lord Shiva the destroyer; Hitler and Mother Teresa. All of it, all of it, all of it.

To single out past lives is to gain the perspective that each of them offers. When you zoom the camera back and you realize that you *are* it all, you gain tremendous compassion. In this expanded identity you can no longer separate yourself from those you judge against or the saviors to whom you deflect your holiness.

The story is told that when Leonardo da Vinci set out to paint his famous depiction of the Last Supper, he searched Florence for subjects who embodied the character of his biblical subjects. The genius painter began with a tall handsome man who bore the stature and purity of Christ. Then, after years of setting the images of the other disciples to canvas, Leonardo was ready to paint the traitor Judas. He searched ardently for a tortured soul, and eventually found a dirty, agonized prisoner in a dungeon. When Leonardo asked the man if he would sit for a portrait, the fellow asked, "Don't you remember me?"

"I don't think so," answered the artist, bewildered.

"I sat for your portrait of Jesus," the man answered.

Within every human being is the propensity to rise to the highest of the high, and to sink to the lowest of the low. That is why we can never judge another for their sins or errors. Given the same circumstances, we might take the same action they did and find ourselves in the same predicament. Mother Teresa began her care for abandoned children "on the day I discovered I had a Hitler inside of me."

While we all may also share a propensity to be a Hitler, we more fundamentally share a propensity to be God. Our divinity is the truth about us, our humanness the passing show. If one or many lives have yielded you compassion for others and for yourself, they have served you well. We might even say that the only purpose of one life or many is to live, as the book by Machaelle Small Wright suggests, "as if the God in all life matters."

The Biggest Picture

We are told that the purpose of ongoing reincarnation is to perfect our soul—to sandpaper our rough spots, polish our virtues, break the chain of karma, and escape the need to be born again and again and again.

On one playing field, this may be so. But there is an even greater playing field which, if you understand it, can short-cut the entire process of becoming perfect, and save you eons of struggling, striving, and suffering. The cosmic *aha!* is this: Perfection is not a feat you attain; it is a state you recognize. You will never *become* perfect, but you will come to understand that you are *already* perfect. The secret to getting off the karmic wheel is to realize that the real you was never on it. You subscribed to illusions about yourself that shrank you to a tiny modicum of all you are and made you believe you deserve to suffer. But you can transcend that limiting belief by recognizing that it was only in dreams that you became a mortal body. Upon awakening, one body or many could never contain the real you.

This flash of insight brings us to the reality of Grace. Spiritual master Paramahansa Yogananda declared, "Grace supersedes karma." Even while you believe you have karma to pay off, the Law of Grace declares you debt-free. You are loved, whole, and welcome in the kingdom now, and you need not do anything to redeem yourself. Your redemption has already been accomplished; it is just waiting for you to accept it. Salvation comes not through acts, but through awakening. Know that you are redeemed, and you are. This is where karma ends.*

You are free to return to the world as many times as you like, and you are also free to soar beyond it. If believing in

---

* My book *The Grace Factor* offers an in-depth exploration of the presence and power of grace, and how it frees us from limitation, guilt, and pain.

reincarnation helps you gain the vision of freedom, it is serving you well. If it makes you feel limited, trapped, or owing, it is hurting you. Everything has value only in how we use it. Whether you have one or many bodies is less important than what you do with them. More fundamentally, what you do with your mind determines your destiny.

When you realize that you are bigger than your karma, it can no longer contain you. Jesus gave us many clues about how worthy and powerful we are: "I am here to bring you life more abundant." "Even greater things than I, shall you do." "If you had enough faith, you could say to this mountain, 'Move!' and it would move." Jesus quoted from the Book of Psalms: "You are gods, children of the most high, all of you." These promises are not made to limited, mortal beings, trapped for eons on an excruciating karmic wheel. They are promises to divine beings, urging us to claim our true nature and destiny. How many times you have walked the earth, and who you were, is not nearly as important as who you are now and what you do with the life before you. The universe gives you infinite opportunities to remember your divine identity. The moment you do, everything that has led up to this moment dissolves in the brilliant light of the eternal now.

DIRECT CONNECT 19
Free Now

Do you have a sense of who you might have been in a previous life? If so, who were you and what was that life about?

Does your idea of reincarnation free you, or does it bind you?

Do you believe there are prerequisites you must meet before you can be worthy of peace or freedom?

How long do you believe it will take for you to pay off your karma and attain enlightenment or liberation?

How would you feel and how would you be living differently if you knew you were free now, and did not have to jump through any more hoops or pass any more tests to be worthy of the kingdom of heaven?

CLOSER THAN YOU KNOW

Emmanuel introduced us to a present, loving God, not a distant, pie-in-the-sky, "maybe you can get to heaven if you suffer now" punitive entity. Death, to Emmanuel, is pure fiction. He summed it up: "Death is completely safe."

Emmanuel's teaching reminded me of an incident that occurred when Carla Gordan went to a hospital to visit a friend who was close to passing on. A young woman, Annie, was intensely afraid of dying. During her visit, Carla brought Guide Mary through to interact with Annie. During that conversation, Mary bestowed Annie with a vision of heaven, showing her what she would experience when she reached the other side.

"What do you think about dying now?" Mary asked when the session was done.

Annie replied with a broad smile, "A piece of cake."

We all ponder what will happen when we leave the world, and we all have loved ones who have sailed beyond earthly shores. We wonder how and where they are, and we wish we could communicate with them. We can. People who have died are not very far from us at all. They simply dwell on the other side of a curtain. We can part that curtain and connect with them if we wish.

All of the teachers I introduce in this book, as well as every great spiritual guide, concur on one fact: There is no death. While the body may wither and dissolve, our true self lives on. In that truth we may take comfort when confronting our own passing or that of a loved one.

While you and I have heard all kinds of stories about what happens after we die, many of them frightening, there is far more to the afterlife than we have been led to believe. The most important thing to know about the afterlife is that there is no afterlife. There is only life. Nothing can come after what always is. The forms through which life expresses change, but the energy that expresses through them is unchangeable and eternal. There is so much more to life than the body! The source of life is everywhere, always.

More Than a Body

I had never sat with anyone who was dying. Now my mother lay before me, about to leave this world. Mom took a deep breath in, she breathed out, and she did not breathe in again. That was it. When I realized she was gone, I sat with her for a while. As I studied her inert body, a stunning realization came to me: That body was not my mother. Physically, yes. But there was so much more to her and our relationship than her body or mine. My real mother was the soul who animated that body. That was the person who loved me, cared for me, supported me unconditionally, and was there for me at the crucial turning points in my life. Her body was the vehicle through which she expressed that love. Now her spirit had laid the body aside and moved on. Recognizing that my mother was far more than her body, and that our relationship far transcended our bodies, brought me great comfort.

Earlier I recounted how my mother sent me a *mezuzah* after she passed away. That was but one of many communications I have had with her since she left this world. She often comes to me in dreams, and I sometimes hear her voice offering advice when I have an important decision to make. When I had my sessions with Carla channeling Mary, my mother would often send a message. The energy and content of those messages clearly indicated it was her.

During one reading with Mary, my mother gave me an especially poetic message uncharacteristic of her usual voice. Stunned, I commented to Mary, "Wow, that was really profound. I didn't think my mother would come up such a statement." Mary smiled and replied, "True love brings with it true wisdom."

Where there is love, there is life. Where there is life, there is connection. Where there is connection, there is communication. Your departed loved ones are much closer than you know.

How to Connect

I often coach people who have recently lost a loved one and are in the grieving process. They miss their dear one and wish they could connect with that person, but have not been able to do so. I invite such clients to feel their feelings and express their sadness or grief. Those important emotions are calling for attention and cannot be glossed over. Most people need to go through their grieving before they can come out on the other side.

After the client has expressed his or her feelings and is ready for a next step (immediately or at a later time), I give them a few tips to comfort them and help them make that important connection:

1. Quit saying you "lost" this person. Yes, your loved one is gone physically, and a sense of loss certainly feels real. From a higher perspective, however, they are not gone and you did not lose them. They simply shifted dimensions or, as some say, "changed addresses." If you were unable to contact them, they would be lost. But you can contact them, thus they are available and found.

2. Do whatever you can to raise your vibration so you can meet your departed one at the refined frequency at which they now exist. If you are grieving or immersed in a sense of loss, sorrow, anger, or guilt, you are engulfed in a dense emotional force field your friend in a high place cannot penetrate. When you relax and lighten up, you elevate your frequency to match theirs. Do what brings you joy and lifts or relaxes you, and you will open the door for communication. A walk on the beach, watching a funny movie, or dinner with a dear friend may seem unrelated to your ability to communicate with your loved one, but such activities significantly enhance your availability.

3. Watch for signs. Your loved one may come to you in a dream; her face may appear during a meditation; you might hear his voice whispering to you as you are falling asleep; or you might get a subtle waft of the perfume she wore. Or someone you are talking to may casually use an unusual phrase your loved one used, or mention an odd place your loved one frequented. Don't write off such signs as coincidence. They more likely indicate genuine communication.

4. Create a sacred area honoring your beloved one. People of Asian ancestry set aside an area of their home where they maintain an altar dedicated to their departed ancestors. We westerners would do well to emulate this thoughtful tradition. Place a photo or meaningful memento in your sacred space and keep some flowers or other inspiring objects on it. Light a candle and take a few moments each day to pray or communicate at your altar. This site and your dedicated action create a portal for your loved one to remain in your consciousness and be with you.

5. Do your spiritual practice. Prayer, meditation, yoga, tai chi, *A Course in Miracles,* and similar practices place you in a state of mind that helps you attain a degree of inner peace that lifts you beyond sorrow. In inner quietude you will become more receptive to communication with your beloved, as well as your spirit guides, angels, and other invisible helpers.

6. Write letters to your loved one. Write letters to your loved one as if they will receive and read them. Write down what you sense they would write back to you. Tell them what you would like them to know, and listen for their response. You may be surprised at the clarity of their expression. Such communication is far closer to reality than imagination.

7. Be open to relationships with living people as venues for your beloved to reach you. In some of my seminars I guide an exercise in which participants pair up and gaze at each other quietly and meditatively, accompanied by soft music. Occasionally while a student is looking into his or her partner's eyes, the face of a departed loved one appears, superimposed over the partner's face. This occurs because the participant is in a relaxed, open, meditative state of mind, and the departed person found a window of opportunity to slip in and say hello. Participants who experience this are always moved by the moment of contact. When you spend quality time with people you love and engage in meaningful conversations and activities, you offer your dearly departed a kind of spiritual runway to find their way to Earth to be with you.

8. You might consult with a medium or channel to help facilitate communication. A truly gifted medium serves as a bridge to the other side. Be discerning about the medium or channel you choose. While there are many good mediums, there are also many who profess to be channeling, but are not. Be sure this person is gifted and their practice is established in integrity and service. Speak to the practitioner beforehand, or talk to others who have worked with that person, to confirm that this person is reputable, pure of heart, and connected to a higher source.

9. Indulge in books, movies, and other media that accurately portray interdimensional communication. While many media depictions tend to be spooky or sensational, a small portion are educational and inspiring. The movie *A Rumor of Angels* and the related book *Thy Son Liveth* are examples of stories based on real life positive communication with the departed.

10. Do a release ceremony. By yourself or with one or a few good friends, make a clear statement of release to your loved one. You might write it out beforehand. Tell your dear one that you love them and you now release them to move on with their own spiritual journey. In doing so, you release yourself to get on with your own life.

DIRECT CONNECT 20

A Sample Release Ceremony

By yourself or with one or a few chosen friends, speak words like those below. If it helps, write them out beforehand.

My dear_____, you have been such an important part of my life. I deeply value our connection and the beautiful and even the challenging times we have shared. I will always love and bless your presence in my life.

It is now time for me to let you go. I can no longer carry you in my mind and heart as I have been doing. I must free you and myself.

I now release you to go on with your journey, and I release myself to go on with mine. I trust that we are both embraced in the arms of love and we will be guided. I place you in the hands of God, and allow you to merge into the light.

If you wish to visit or communicate with me, I am open to that. I want the healthy and blessed elements of our relationship to continue. For now, I let go of any attachment to you that has caused me pain, and I cut any spiritual cords that have kept you tethered to me or the world.

I love you, I bless you, and I release you.

And so it is.

Heal through Self-Expression

Many people feel sad, frustrated, guilty, or angry because a loved one passed away before their relationship was complete. Perhaps a divorced parent moved out of your life; or a parent was sick, abusive, alcoholic, or mentally ill; or there was unresolved enmity between the two of you; or you feel guilty that you did not do enough for them during their lifetime or their process of their passing.

Don't worry—the relationship is not over. Because real relationships occur between spiritual beings and not bodies, that person is still available to you in spirit. You can complete conversations you did not have when that person lived. Even if you do not believe that the person is still alive as a separate entity in spirit, they are still alive in your mind, where the relationship exists. In either case, you can continue communicating with that person until you come to a sense of resolution and find inner peace.

Here are three ways you can do this:

1. Journal your feelings. Some of your frustration after a loved one's departure may accrue due to the thoughts, feelings, and words you did not express to them. Or perhaps you said or did things you regret. While some of your unresolved issues were interpersonal, they are more *intra*personal—less about what was going on between the two of you, and more about what was going on *within* you. You can make significant progress toward resolution by expressing the feelings, both positive and negative, pent up inside you.

Find a quiet space and write down everything you think and feel about this person and your relationship, including what happened during their life, their process of passing, and afterward. Hold nothing back. This is not the time to be polite, "spiritual," or appropriate. It is the time to be honest and to clear the clogged pipeline. If your loved one was a parent who criticized or stifled you for expressing yourself, the journaling exercise will be especially helpful, as it provides an opportunity for you to break free of a lifelong limiting pattern.

If the relationship you are addressing was distressing, you may be tempted to dwell on your upsets. Certainly attend to them, but then go beyond them. Express your feelings of love and appreciation, whether they are few or many. (Often when you acknowledge the few, you will find there were many.) Be honest and generous in expressing gratitude. You loved that person more than you know. Allow that love to come forth, and you will find healing for your soul. It is not the love we do not receive that hurts us; it is the love we do not give.

Keep going in your journal until you have recorded every thought and feeling you can think of. When you do, you will feel purged and relieved. Let the experience sink in so you can absorb its benefits. You can symbolically burn your journal paper afterward or delete your computer file.

2. Talk to a coach, counselor, therapist, or friend. Such a conversation provides an outlet similar to journaling, and may be even more profound because you are sharing and exposing your feelings to another person. If you choose someone who loves you or has coaching skills, you will find that they accept you with your upsets and weighty feelings, and they do not judge or reject you. This forgiveness will offset the judgment and rejection you imposed upon yourself or your loved one. The counselor or friend does not need to offer you advice. You may simply need a compassionate listening ear.

3. In meditation or prayer, call this person to you and tell them what you would like them to know. Focus on their name or face until you sense their presence. You may even see them clearly in your mind's eye. Acknowledge your love for them and your desire for them to remain with you and continue your communication, if you wish. Leave nothing unspoken, and imagine that the recipient will receive your communication. He or she will.

After you have spoken your piece, listen for their response. You can have a rich and fulfilling conversation with them. Keep communicating until you feel a sense of release and resolution. I have done this exercise myself and guided many people through it. When done with sincere intention, the results are cleansing and healing.

This practice does not have to be a one-time experience. You can create an ongoing conversation with this person. You are reinventing your connection, which will continue to your mutual reward if you both wish.

Even though my parents passed away a long time ago, my relationship with them is very much alive and continually evolving. The great illusion is that we are bodies only, and what happens to the body happens to us. More fundamentally we are spirits, and what happens to our spirit happens to us. Because love is forever, so are our relationships. It is the destiny of all relationships to resolve in peace, with or without bodies.

Your Healing Benefits Your Departed Loved Ones

When you take a step toward resolving your relationship with those on the other side, you contribute to their healing as well as yours. They want to resolve your relationship as much as you do. Your souls' journeys are intertwined. You chose to be together for mutual growth. When you use your relationship to advance spiritually, you enable them to do the same.

In the touching movie *Heart and Souls*, a little boy named Thomas has five spirit guides who stay close to him and constantly help him. Thomas's parents ridicule him for believing in "invisible friends," and as he grows older he becomes immersed in worldly pursuits and forgets about them. At a crucial moment in Thomas's adulthood when he desperately needs help, his guides reappear and urge him to connect with certain people in the world for reasons he does not understand. Thomas initially resists, but then complies. Eventually we see that the connections the spirit guides want Thomas to make help not only him, but aid them to complete their own unresolved relationships. *A Course in Miracles* calls us to remember, "When I am healed, I am not healed alone." This key dynamic applies not only to our relationships with people in the physical world, but to people in worlds beyond, as well.

Overcoming Survivor Guilt

Many people who live on after the passing of a loved one feel bad or wrong for remaining alive while the other person is not. This makes no sense and should not be indulged in the least. Your beloved who has gone on had their date with destiny; it is no accident when they left. *A Course in Miracles* tells us, "Chance plays no part in God's plan." All death occurs at a level of choice far deeper than the thinking mind can fathom. So does life. If you are still here, you have a divinely appointed purpose. You continue to express in the world for important reasons that benefit you and others. You will exit stage left in your own right timing, and you will be reunited with your loved ones at that time.

Don't use the passing of a loved one as an excuse to wallow in self-pity, self-doubt, depression, or emotional inertia. Grieve as much as you need to, but then get on with your life. Ask yourself, "Would_____ want me to be sad and crawl into a hole, or would he or she want me to be happy?" Your loved one wants you to move on and live your best possible life. Your sadness or pain does not honor that person. Your joy and success do.

Undoing Relief Guilt

Perhaps, upon hearing about someone's passing, you are glad this person does not walk the Earth anymore. This sounds like a terrible thing to think, since we are supposed to want everyone to live and prosper. But many people who have had a painful, abusive, or conflict-ridden relationship feel a sense of relief when the person who troubled them dies. If you feel this way about anyone, you don't need to feel ashamed or guilty. This feeling provides a platform for two significant pieces of spiritual work:

First, forgive yourself for being relieved about someone dying. In a sense, this feeling demonstrates that your spiritual guidance is working well. It is unnatural and unhealthy to participate in a painful relationship. If your relationship was characterized by abuse or conflict, your inner being was screaming, "This can't be it! I was not meant to live like this!" Even though you may have accepted the struggle for reasons that seemed justified at the time, the mistreatment continued to grate against your soul. Turmoil is *supposed to* grate against your soul to motivate you to take action to correct it. If you settled for a bad relationship, the situation continued to call for resolution.

When the person with whom you had conflict dies, your sense of relief represents your inner being saying, "I'm glad this situation is out of my life. I didn't and don't deserve that experience." That person's death is symbolic that that dysfunctional energy has moved out of your sphere of experience. So, it is not really the person whose death brings you relief; it is the death of participating in conflict.

A Course in Miracles teaches that guilt is never an appropriate response to any situation. No matter what your church or parents told you, guilt is not of God. It is a human invention, perpetrated by the ego. People judge; God forgives. People cling; God releases. Whatever you feel guilty about, you are not seeing clearly. Guilt does not remove pain from our experience; it perpetuates it. Loving and accepting yourself even if you are glad someone has died is the first step to healing yourself and your relationship with that person.

The second spiritual benefit of such a sense of relief is that it signals that you still have some work to do with that person or what they symbolize to you. It is the destiny of all relationships to complete in love; until they do, some illusion is preventing you from seeing yourself and the other person clearly. The false limiting belief must be confronted and peeled away. Pain in any relationship, with the living or dead, is a call for forgiveness. Forgiveness does not mean that you should accept abuse, condone it, deny it, or make believe it is right. It means that you take back the power you attributed to that person or their actions. You claim your right to live a happy, healthy, empowered life no matter what they did. You rise above a victim mentality, undo fear, guilt, or resistance, and move on. You look beyond the behavior and see the inner person who was wounded, like a hurt child, and you strive to replace hatred with compassion. You can't bypass forgiveness. Until you forgive, you remain in emotional jail with the person you hate.

Forgiveness is a gift to yourself. When you release the other person, you release yourself. One way to achieve forgiveness is to reframe the other person as a teacher with whom you had a soul contract to help you grow. They forced you to find inner strength you would not have found had your relationship been easier. Perhaps you learned to honor yourself, refuse to participate in dysfunction, or set healthy boundaries. The soul growth we gain from transforming painful relationships often outshines the soul growth we gain from joyful relationships, which bless us in a different way. *A Course in Miracles* tells us, "The holiest spot on earth is where an ancient hatred has become a present love."

Your feelings of relief about someone passing are not random and they are not a cause for judgment. They are an arrow pointing you toward the door of healing.

Nineteen Again

My mentor Hilda saw departed spirits as regularly and familiarly as you and I see physical bodies. She explained that such people emanate the exuberance and vitality of a nineteen-year-old person. When the pain, restriction, and creaking of an aging or ill body are put aside, that person returns to their natural state as a radiant spiritual being. I have heard numerous psychics and mediums confirm this description. They don't mean that that the person is literally nineteen years old, since in spirit there is no time and no age. They are using the age to describe a phase of life when most people are at the height of their aliveness, enthusiasm, and hopeful vision. You don't need to wait until you die to become nineteen again. You can tap into that glorious feeling at any age and sustain it for a lifetime. We all know people who are elderly but vital, playful, and exuberant. The vision of a youthful spirit provides an empowering model of who we are when the body is laid aside, which we can also enjoy until the body is laid aside.

Who Gets into Heaven

Channeled entities Emmanuel, Abraham, and Bashar teach that everyone goes to heaven. Leaving the physical world, they explain, is like stepping out of a movie. The moment the lights go on, all the images on the screen disappear, including the good guys, bad guys, and all the weird or violent things that went on in the movie, which was but a play of light and shadows. As much as we would like to think that bad guys get sent you-know-where when they go to the other side, these teachers say that isn't so. The ego craves "poetic justice," but the spirit craves healing. Jesus taught the Law of Grace, which supersedes the law of karma. Karma goes on in the movie. Grace goes on when you exit the theater. Grace is the ultimate justice.

If the bad guys don't get punished, neither do you. You go home to the loving arms of God. This teaching will not sit well with religions that depend on threats of eternal hell to scare you into following dogma. But when during life you act in ways that bring pain, you are *already* in hell. Hell is not just the result of evil acts; it is the *cause* of them. Fear compels people to hurt others, and fear is hell. People who do evil are punished before, during, and after their evil act, even while they walk the earth; not by God, but by the universal principle that when we live out of alignment with Spirit, we feel bad. I guarantee you that Hitler was not a happy camper. For a human being, or others like him, to perpetrate the heinous acts he spawned, he had to live in deep agony. Evil is self-punishing in the moment an evil act is perpetrated. The appearance of worldly power or success is no indicator of inner peace. It is often a contra-indicator.

If the world is a stage on which each of us plays our part, as Shakespeare noted, what happens on the stage is unrelated to what happens off the stage. Great actors sometimes play good guys and sometimes they play bad guys. Truly talented actors take on versatile characters. Some actors who have played villains for decades turn to light-hearted comedy roles. Some comedians break out of being type-cast and take dramatic roles. Just as actors are not their fictional characters, we are not the parts we play in the movie of the world. Ultimately, we all leave the stage and come home. As an Italian proverb tells, "When the chess game is over, the king and the pawn go back into the same box."

Reinvent Your Identity

After my coaching client Marci's husband passed away, she became entrenched in her identity as a widow. Dark clothing dominated her wardrobe, her personality was muted, she hardly went out, and she adopted a victim story about her husband's passing. I could practically see a sign pasted on Marci's forehead: Widow. This identity was not serving Marci, but was limiting her from living her fullest life. I told Marci that it appeared that she was hiding behind her widow identity as an excuse to avoid diving back into life. I asked her if she would be willing to let go of her widow story and emerge as a new person in the now. Marci admitted that she had gotten into a rut over the years and she wanted to get out of it. Marci got rid of her widow clothing, began to socialize and date, and eventually married a wonderful guy with whom she now has a soul-fulfilling relationship.

It's not what happens to us that makes or breaks our life; it's how we think about it. The death of a loved one can be one of the most difficult experiences of a lifetime. We all feel the burden of such a loss, and we need time to regroup. Yet at some point we reach a crossroads: We can either become entrenched in a sense of deprivation, or we can shift our vision toward new possibilities. We can hide out in pain, or use it as a motivation to step forward. Eventually we can and must move on. How long that takes, and how hard the process is, is up to each of us. May we all use our relationships with our loved ones, in this world and beyond it, to enhance our life, not detract from it.

Faith, Comfort, and Healing

The most important gift of receiving messages from departed loved ones is not the information that comes through. It is the deep soul comfort of knowing that our loved ones are still with us. The illusion of death makes it appear that people we love are gone forever. It is not so. The people you love are with you always. True love does not depend on the proximity of bodies. Bodies die, but relationships are forever. Genuine mediums and channelers give us faith that there is more to life than our physical eyes look upon.

Ultimately you do not need a psychic or medium to bridge the gap between worlds. Such a professional can serve well when you are immersed in loss and you need faith. Eventually you can develop direct relationships with those in spirit rather than going through an intermediary. Your loved ones yearn to connect with you as much as you yearn to connect with them. Life goes on far longer than bodies, and love never dies.

DIRECT CONNECT 21
Closer Than You Know

If someone you love has passed on, how are you dealing with their departure?

If you could communicate directly with your loved one, what would you say to them?

What do you believe they would say to you in response?

If you are grieving, how might you raise your vibration so you can make yourself more accessible to communicate with your loved one?

Have you had any signs, synchronicities, or communication from your loved one? If so, what were those messages and what do they mean to you?

How can you live in a way that honors your loved one and your ongoing relationship with them?

PART VI

ABRAHAM:

WE'RE ALL IN THIS TOGETHER

HOW ATTRACTIVE YOU ARE

I opened my mailbox to find a small yellow padded envelope from a sender I did not recognize. Inside I found a white cassette tape with a blue label accompanied by a note: "We thought you would enjoy this seminar recording. Abraham tells a story similar to one you told." The message was from Jerry Hicks, husband of Esther Hicks, who speaks for the nonphysical teacher Abraham.

I popped the cassette in my player and heard Abraham recall a day when Jerry and Esther got stuck in a traffic jam on New York's Tappan Zee Bridge. With traffic at a standstill, motorists were upset and issuing New York expletives. By contrast, Jerry and Esther decided to simply enjoy the day and had a great deal of fun connecting with other motorists waiting for the jam to clear.

Jerry had read an article I wrote about the day I was en route to the San Francisco airport and had gotten bogged in traffic on the Bay Bridge. Although at first I felt distraught and feared I might miss my plane, I decided to use the moment to savor the spring day. I looked out my window and smiled and waved at some kids and a dog in the RV beside me. I relaxed and quit worrying about my flight, which I eventually made with time to spare. Abraham and I came to the same moral of the story: *No place is worth getting to unless you enjoy the ride to get there.*

Abraham went on to describe the Law of Attraction and how we draw people and events to us by virtue of the thoughts and feelings we dwell on. While I had heard about the Law of Attraction from other metaphysical teachers, Abraham illuminated it with fresh authority and simplicity. I wanted to hear more from Abraham and learn how to use the Law of Attraction in my favor. I ordered more recordings, which initiated a deeply rewarding relationship between me, Esther, Jerry, and their invisible guide Abraham.

A few months later I found myself in Texas enjoying dinner with Jerry and Esther in their home outside San Antonio. I found them to be bright, upbeat, fun-loving people dedicated to sharing and living the teachings of Abraham. We had endless things to talk about, and I knew these were soul friends with whom I was reuniting.

Abraham Appears

In the mid-1980's, Jerry and Esther decided to try meditation. After a few minutes' practice, Esther felt a pleasant numbness, almost tingly. Soon her numbness gave way to buoyancy to the point that she couldn't feel her chair, as if she was floating. Then she felt as if some force was "breathing" her. The experience was blissful, ecstatic, and a little frightening.

Esther and Jerry continued their meditation practice for nine months, until Esther noticed her head moving around during the sessions. Then she realized her head was moving in a pattern, her nose writing in the air. She told Jerry, and the two became excited. The nose spelled, "I am Abraham.

I am your spiritual guide. I love you. I am here to work with you."

This "nose-writing" went on for a few months, Jerry recording the words that came. Then one night in bed Esther found her hands thumping on Jerry's chest. "That's not me," Esther realized, and surmised that Abraham wanted to write through her. She went to a keyboard and wrote automatically, "iwanttotypeiwanttotypeiwanttotype . . ." This phrase went on for an entire page, motivating Esther to continue. For the following few months, Abraham's messages came through in the written word.

Then, while driving on the freeway, the couple found themselves in a middle lane, sandwiched between two 18-wheeler trucks. Esther, frightened, felt her jaw wanting to move. She let it, and the words, "Take the next exit," came out. This was the first time Abraham spoke orally through Esther.

The couple, still shy about the process of channeling, kept it mostly to themselves for about a year. Then they began to share Abraham's teachings with a handful of people, which led to small gatherings until, over time, the sessions became popular. Knowledge of Abraham snowballed until seminar attendance became huge, Jerry and Esther travelling all around the world delivering Abraham's message to millions of people who have found upliftment and experienced many positive life changes.

All in This Together

I had the pleasure to connect with Esther and Jerry several times a year. Whenever we were in the same city, we would meet for dinner and speak of many things personal and spiritual. Even while Abraham-Hicks (the name they chose for their company, representing that the messages were a collaboration of the energies brought by both Abraham and the Hicks) was becoming a sensation, the couple maintained their humility and down-home nature.

Occasionally a topic would come up during dinner that would puzzle us. Esther would stop the conversation and say, "Let's hear what Abraham has to say about this." She closed her eyes, and Abraham came through with an illuminating message.

Once, when I had a personal question for Abraham, Esther brought Abraham through with an answer. Afterward I told Abraham, "Thanks so much. That answer was very helpful."

Abraham smiled coyly and replied, "We are all in this together."

As I have pondered that simple statement over many years, its meaning has run deeper for me. Why would an enlightened spirit guide say, "We are all in this together?" Surely a bodyless, deathless, illuminated master like Abraham would not be in the same "this" as the rest of us struggling, suffering human beings. Yet Abraham was teaching a lesson in compassion and unity. Abraham is not separate from us, a perfect god sitting on a lofty distant throne. Abraham is an aspect of our own self, moving through the journey of spiritual evolution. Likewise, none of us can separate ourselves and see ourselves as above or below another person, closer to God or farther. We must help each other wherever we can to rise beyond the fear and misunderstanding that has carved humanity's sorrows. We must ascend to claim our identity as divine beings.

Are You as Enlightened as Your Dog?

I once asked Abraham, "Has there ever been a being who has walked the earth and remained in a full state of enlightenment?"

Abraham smiled and answered, "Your dog."

Abraham initially knew about my dog Munchie through my book *Are You as Happy as Your Dog?* Later, when Esther and Jerry visited my home, they met my beloved furry companion. Abraham's answer to my question was not referring to my dog only, but to the state of consciousness in which most dogs live.

"Dogs have very simple needs and their minds are not cluttered with thoughts, fears, and resistance, like human beings," Abraham went on. "They remain connected to Source energy and, unless mistreated, live in a constant state of joy."

At another time a fellow in Abraham's audience said, "I know this is a silly question, but I will ask it anyway: Why do dogs love to ride in cars with their head sticking out the window?"

Abraham replied, "That's not a silly question at all. It is actually the best question we have ever heard. Dogs love to ride with their head out the window for the pure joy of it. It feels good and it's fun. They need no more reason than that. Humans, on the other hand, rarely do things for pure joy. You believe you have to earn your happiness and justify it through self-deprivation and sacrifice. Dogs have none of that. In finding immense pleasure in the ride, they are fulfilling their purpose to experience and express joy—which is your purpose too."

That answer provides a neat summary of Abraham's teachings. We are here not to struggle or suffer. We are here to be happy and express our unique self. When we are connected to Source energy, well-being flows through us and out to the world. The entire journey of life leads to this glorious recognition and expression.

The Law of Attraction, Simplified

While many people strive to become attractive, they do not realize that they are already totally attractive. At every moment we draw to us people, events, and situations equivalent to the thoughts, feelings, and attitudes we dwell in. There is a perfect correlation between what we believe and what we are getting. While we may argue that a person or circumstance showed up out of the blue, unrelated to our consciousness, it is not so. The thoughts we focus on generate our experience. To change our experience, we must examine and change our thoughts. When we upgrade our beliefs and feelings to match our intentions, we attain spiritual mastery.

There are two levels at which the Law of Attraction plays out. The first is at the level of our perception. Because the world "out there" is a projection of the mindset we are using to see it, when we change our mindset, we change our vision of the world and our experience of it. So the most fundamental use of the Law of Attraction is to consciously choose the thoughts through which we view the world. When we change *the way* we see, we change *what* we see.

The second application of the Law of Attraction is that when we upgrade our perception, people, things, and situations show up in the physical world that demonstrate our change of mind. This is the miracle level of manifestation: individuals, connections, and events come to us that we could not possibly orchestrate though conscious manipulation.

My client Jeff had a longstanding acrimonious relationship with his ex-wife Marla. The couple had gone through a rocky divorce, their communication was hostile, and they continued to fight over child care. In coaching, Jeff told me, "This relationship is so hard for me. I am so angry, I can't sleep, and I have physical symptoms from the stress. I can't go on like this."

I asked Jeff to close his eyes and imagine Marla standing before him. As he started to fidget, I encouraged him to stay with the exercise. "Now look into Marla's eyes and see if you can find the light in her. Look for the person you loved when you married her. Find the place in your heart that values your relationship. Make an effort to accept and appreciate her, for even a moment."

Jeff took a deep breath, and after a few moments his face lightened up. His shoulders relaxed and he grew more peaceful. I invited him to sit with that feeling for a little while.

After the exercise he told me, "At first I had a hard time connecting with Marla. But then I got to a place where I remembered the good in her and let her into my heart."

Later that day I received a phone call from Jeff. "You won't believe what happened!" he spouted. "I went to pick up my daughter from Marla's house, and she asked me to sit with her for a bit. She told me, 'I have been thinking about our relationship. I want it to be better. I don't want to be at odds with you anymore. You are a good man. I'm sorry for my part in our upsets. Let's start over and, even though we have taken different paths, I want our relationship to be supportive and harmonious.'

"I almost fell on the floor," Jeff told me. "I was so happy to hear that from her. I told her that I wanted the same, and let's do what we can to get along and give our daughter the best role model of parents that we can."

I consider this event the result of a scientific experiment. The only thing that changed was that for a moment Jeff held his ex-wife in positive regard. When something inside Jeff changed, he stimulated something in Marla to change. This was not just a change in perception; it was a tangible, demonstrable change in events triggered by a change in perception.

Immersed in the Mindset

Actor Jim Carrey understood the Law of Attraction when in 1985 he wrote himself a "play" check in the amount of ten million dollars for "acting services rendered," dated 1995. He had nowhere near that amount of money in his bank account at the time, but this was his act of faith to stimulate his career. Ten years later, in 1995, he landed a role in the film *Dumb and Dumber*, for which he received a real check for ten million dollars.

The Bible tells us, "As you think, so shall you be." Thought always precedes manifestation. Things are thoughts made solid. Every solid object you see is a projection of your thought about it. To attempt to improve manifestation by manipulating objects at a logistical level only is fruitless. The outside world changes only when you change your mind. Ultimately you don't need to change the world. You simply need to change your mind.

Abraham-Hicks has made a huge contribution to elevating my consciousness and the lives of many. They have attained more notoriety than many other spiritual teachers and legitimized communication with the nonphysical for millions of people who might otherwise doubt or deny it. Many people are now aware of the Law of Attraction and are striving to use it in their favor. I deeply appreciate the contribution of Esther, Jerry (who has now passed on), and Abraham, as important guides on my path, and remarkable uplifters of humanity. You can find a wealth of their recordings, books, and Abraham's ongoing events at www. abraham-hicks.com

DIRECT CONNECT 22
Attraction in Action

Consider a positive, rewarding relationship or situation in your life. What thoughts, beliefs, or attitudes attracted this person or situation to you?

Consider a negative or depleting relationship or situation in your life. What thoughts, beliefs, or attitudes attracted this person or situation to you?

Can you accept full responsibility for the situations you have attracted, so you gain the power to attract situations by your choice in the future?

What can you do to immerse your mind, feelings, and experience in the ideal situation(s) you would like to attract?

PROPHETS AND DEFICITS

My coaching client Sheila sat before me, mascara running down her cheeks. A fortune teller had told her that she would marry a lawyer from the U.K., he would cheat on her, and the couple would bitterly divorce. After I did what I could to calm the hysterical woman, I explained that while some psychic predictions are accurate, she can make choices that steer her destiny rather than be prey to a dire fate laid upon her. I assured her that she can access her own inner guidance instead of depending on an outer voice to tell her what will happen. That coaching session occurred fifteen years ago; since that time no such incident has occurred. The fortune teller was reading Sheila's fear more than her destiny.

Abraham does not make many prophecies. They* prefer to anchor students in alignment with self now. We must accept responsibility to create the future we prefer by making wise choices right where we stand. Like all the teachers in this book, Abraham seeks to create masters, not disciples.

---

*Abraham prefers to be addressed in the plural, indicating that the name we may think of as one entity really represents a consortium of entities and energies speaking through one voice.

A farmer had three lazy sons who did not participate in cultivating the family's crops. On his deathbed, the farmer told his sons that he had buried an extremely valuable treasure in one of his fields. But the farmer died before he could tell the sons where the treasure was located. Eager to find the fortune, the sons began to dig up the fields. Since the family had large acreage, they worked hard to turn over every inch of the sprawling springtime grounds. After weeks of laboriously digging and sifting, they did not find any treasure. Disappointed, they went ahead and planted crops as they had seen their father do. That fall the farm yielded the most abundant and profitable crop the family had ever seen, due to the well-cultivated soil. The sons were so pleased with the result that they went on to become skilled farmers, and produced larger and richer crops each year. The treasure the father was referring to was not a chest of gold. It was the benefit the sons would receive by participating in creating healthy, abundant crops.

It is tempting to go to a psychic to tell you how to live and what the future will bring. Good psychics provide very helpful information. Yet the best psychics do not simply tell you what to do. More important, they help you understand the dynamics behind your decisions so you can make wise choices for yourself. The real treasure comes from digging up your own answers. When you learn how to get where you want to go, you are empowered far more than if someone takes you there.

I was once invited on short notice to be a guest on a radio show interview. The host had originally scheduled another guest who cancelled shortly before the program, and I was taking his place. When the host began to take phone calls from listeners, they asked me specific questions: "When will I meet my soulmate?" "Should I move to Chicago?" and "Where is my lost cat?" It didn't take long for me to figure out that the guest I replaced was a psychic. Listeners had read the program description and thought I was the psychic giving on-air readings.

At first, I simply told the listeners that I was not a psychic. Then I began to coach them as I usually coach my clients. I used their questions not to give them quick answers, but to stimulate their self-discovery. "What is happening inside you that keeps you from meeting your soulmate, and how can you open up to attract and be satisfied with someone?" "Would you prefer to move to Chicago or stay where you are?" "What does your cat mean to you and what can you do to find her?" I helped the listeners shine light on their own solutions rather than me telling them what to do. In accessing their inner wisdom, they gained skills that would serve them far more than if I had given them a quick answer.

The same Source that will give a psychic information about your life, will give *you* information about your life. You may not initially be in touch with your knowing, but it is there. A good psychic or counselor helps you gain access to your own knowing. The recognition of your divine connection is the greatest gift a teacher can give you.

Psychic Ladders

Working with a psychic, or being one, can be intriguing, illuminating, and extremely helpful. Such interactions can also be fraught with distractions and pitfalls. In this chapter we will explore how to work with a psychic counselor so you derive the highest benefit. If you are a psychic, counselor, or healer, this will also provide you with a framework to maintain your practice at the highest level of integrity.

Let's begin with the positive potential of getting or giving a psychic reading:

1. A psychic can help you become aware of beliefs, behaviors, or patterns within you that are creating beneficial or harmful results. As a result of expanded awareness, you can make healthy choices and save time and trouble on your learning curve. A qualified counselor can help accelerate your personal, professional, and spiritual advancement.

2. A good psychic can train you to access your own inner guidance. Guide Mary confirmed the intuitive guidance I had been receiving, but did not fully trust. Her sessions affirmed that my inner teacher had already been speaking to me loud and clear. Mary helped me gain the confidence to listen to my own higher voice.

My friend Dougall Fraser, an acclaimed psychic counselor, had the courage and humor to write a book with a brilliant title: *But You Knew That Already*. This represents Dougall's integrity, as he teaches his clients that they have access to the information they come to him for.

A psychic with worthy character strives to make his or her clients self-reliant. Yet a psychic with such noble intention will never lack clients. People who strive for genuine spiritual growth will find their way to that counselor's door and return often.

3. A good psychic (or any channeler, astrologer, numerologist, card reader, or esoteric practitioner) uses readings as a venue to help clients learn universal spiritual principles. The session is not so much about delivering information or giving advice as it is about educating the client about how life works and how he or she can live at the highest octave. Thus the client deepens his or her relationship with Higher Power. In this sense, the psychic serves as a spiritual teacher, which goes far beyond reading the client's thoughts, energies, or future.

4. In an emergency or crisis situation, a psychic can offer specific advice to solve the issue at hand. If someone is standing at a crucial crossroads or in danger of making a poor decision, an astute psychic can point the client in a direction and save time and trouble. Later the psychic can help the client understand how that situation fits into the broader picture of his or her life.

5. A good medium can help a client connect with a loved one who has passed on. Such a service provides immense comfort to one who grieves or misses the departed relative or friend. A psychic can also give a client tools to maintain the client's communication with the departed person after the psychic reading. To know that our dear ones are still with us and we can contact them is not simply a comfort for the soul, but a leap in spiritual awakening.

Psychic Chutes

Now let's look at the possible pitfalls or dangers of working with a psychic:

1. The psychic may be only partially accurate or not accurate at all. No psychic, even the best in the profession, is 100% accurate. If a client accepts everything the psychic says as absolute truth, the client may be led down unnecessary, distracting, or harmful byways.

Here are some reasons inaccurate information may come through:

- The psychic is not tapped into a genuine source. Just as you must have your radio tuner set to the station you desire, if the psychic's tuner is not well dialed in, he is going to come up with inaccurate or irrelevant information. If the psychic is not getting any information, he may simply guess incorrectly.

- The psychic's personality is getting in the way. If a counselor has strong personality biases, judgments, or negative influences, or has not risen beyond her personality while giving a reading, she will perceive and interpret in distorted ways.

- The psychic is getting information for someone else. I once went for a psychic reading with a friend. At the time, a tooth was bothering me. As I sat in the room while my friend received her reading, the psychic asked her, "Is your tooth hurting?" The psychic was giving an accurate reading, but not for the client sitting in front of her. You don't need to be in the same room for a psychic to get information about someone else and deliver it as if it applies to you. The other person could be emotionally connected to you or intimately involved in your life.

- The psychic tells you what you want to hear so you will be pleased and return for more readings.

- The psychic is a fraud. While there are many good psychics, there are also fakes who seek to capitalize on vulnerable clients. Let the buyer beware.

2. The psychic may foster the client's dependence on the psychic. Some psychics thrive on dependent personalities. Others simply seek to keep the client coming back to keep their income stream going. Creating false need is never a healthy element in any profession.

A friend of mine is a Tarot card reader who signed up to work on a psychic hotline service. He told me that every technique he was taught by the service was about how to keep the clients on the phone as long as possible to run up their bill. The service gave my friend no training in how to give accurate readings or serve the clients. The entire business was about parting the clients from their shekels.

3. The psychic may attribute undue power to dark forces. Scaring clients with demonic stories creates fear, drama, and subservience to external sources and illusions.

4. The psychic may not honor the client's free will and predict a destiny beyond the client's control. Remember Sheila, the client I mentioned above, who was bent out of shape because a fortune teller told her she was going to marry a lawyer who would cheat on her, and they would get divorced. The subject of my coaching session with that client shifted from her possible disastrous marriage to why she gives her power away to fortune tellers, and how to take it back.

5. The psychic may not respect the client's boundaries. One day I saw my friend, a palm reader, at the beach. She took my hand and began to give me a reading. I withdrew my hand and told her politely, "Thank you, but I don't accept unsolicited readings." A mature psychic either refrains from reading indiscriminately, or asks the client's permission.

Prophecy

History reveals many prophets who have accurately predicted specific events. Heeding helpful prophecies can save us time and trouble, and ignoring them can prove tragic.

While the renowned psychic Jean Dixon was visiting the Ambassador Hotel in Los Angeles in 1968, she predicted that presidential candidate Robert Kennedy would not become President because of a tragedy that would occur at that very site. Later that year Kennedy was shot and killed after he delivered a campaign speech at that hotel. Was this sorrowful event a possibility that could have been averted, or was it destiny?

Of the many personal and global prophecies I have heard from various teachers, psychics, and channelers, only a small portion have come true. While Jean Dixon predicted numerous events that occurred, she also made predictions that did not come to pass. To understand why some predictions come true and others do not, we must look into how prophecy works.

Guide Mary explained, "We [spirit guides] have two weaknesses. The first is prophecy. We can state what we believe is going to happen based on the intention we sense within you. If you wish to walk through a particular doorway, and you are headed in that direction, and the doorway is open, then we will predict that you are going to pass through that door. But if you change your mind or an element of the greater picture alters, that event may not come about."

Bashar (whom we will meet in a later chapter) explains prophecies in terms of probabilities: "No future event is set in stone. At best we can look at how probable it will be for an event to occur. If the probability is high, we will say it will most likely happen. But even if an event is 90% probable, the other 10% could be a deciding factor."

There is one more crucial element in prophecy that we must understand: Sometimes the very act of prophesying an event can alter its outcome. If someone receives a daunting prophecy that motivates the person to change direction, the prophecy is no longer valid. If, for example, a psychic tells a client that his poor health habits are leading to a dire illness, the prediction may get the client's attention. As a result of the forecast, the client improves his health practices and the illness does not come about. In this sense, the prophecy was correct based on the situation at the time the prophecy was given, but the delivered information changed the dynamics so the predicted event was cancelled out.

Decades ago marine biologists predicted that if we continued commercial whaling, within a short time our magnificent aquatic friends would become extinct. As a result of that prediction, ecological groups and governments rallied to ban whaling and other human interferences with the whales' well-being. As a result, the downward trend reversed and whales are now proliferating. A skeptic might argue that the biologists' prophecy was erroneous because whales are now thriving. But it was precisely *because* of the prediction that the whales are now thriving. It was accurate at the time it was issued, but it turned out to be a game-changer rather than a predictor. Thus, negative prophecies can become positive when we use them as wake-up calls.

DIRECT CONNECT 23
Profiting from Prophecies

Have you received one or more prophecies from a psychic, channeler, or medium?

If so, did the information turn out to be true?

If the prediction came true, what did you learn from the experience?

> If the information turned out to not be true, what did you learn from the experience?
>
> What do you believe is your role in creating your destiny?
>
> How much of your life is determined by some outside force, and how much is determined by your choice?

Which Reality?

Another way to understand how prophecy works is to recognize simultaneous parallel realities. All possible events and experiences exist now and always, each within its own reality. Jesus stated, "In my Father's house there are many mansions." A reality exists in which you marry person A, have a family, and go on to live all the extensions of that choice. Meanwhile a reality also exists in which you marry person B, or stay single, or choose another relationship path. (For a brilliant depiction of this dynamic, watch the film *Sliding Doors*.) When a psychic predicts that an event will occur, he is tapping into the reality that matches that event. Meanwhile altogether different realities exist that include all kinds of other events. So the prediction is not based on the notion that there is just one reality, and that is what's going to happen. It is based on the reality you are likely to choose among several or many.

In the classic film *It's a Wonderful Life,* despondent George Bailey, contemplating suicide, wishes he had never been born. George's guardian angel takes him into an alternate reality in which he had not been born and the world is a far darker place for his absence. The vision is so frightening to George that he deeply yearns to reclaim the life he was trying to leave, but now realizes it wasn't so bad. He chooses to return to the life he knew, even with its challenges. It was, after all, a wonderful life. This well-known dramatization teaches that we have a choice about the reality we inhabit. Every thought we think, feeling we indulge, word we speak, and action we take establishes us in the domain that matches our intention. Take care what you focus on, for that sets you up for what you will experience.

If you find yourself in a distasteful reality, don't despair. At any moment you can shift realities. You know how night-time dreams can change in an instant. At one moment you are walking in a garden, then a fox shows up and morphs into a bear, and then you are back in your elementary school classroom, and so on. Nighttime dreams turn on a dime because in that domain you are in the world of the mind only. As mind changes, so does experience. The physical world operates on the same principle, just denser and slower. You can be in love with someone one minute, and out of love the next. You can be wealthy, and then not. You can be healthy and then not, and then healthy again. Anything can change to anything, and you can change it at will. It seems that the external world is creating itself, or is being generated by people and forces outside you. Meanwhile you are the one generating it. To accept this power and responsibility is the key to masterful living.

A prophesy is simply a photograph, a moment frozen in time that represents the state of your mind, body, or world when the photograph is taken. It indicates where things stand or where they are headed. Meanwhile there are a myriad of factors that can change the stream of events so that if another photo were taken down the road, it would show an entirely different picture. I know numerous people who have had x-rays taken showing a seriously diseased organ, and then they engaged in a prayer or healing regime. They returned to the doctor and a new x-ray showed no disease at all. Each x-ray depicted a reflection of the patient's consciousness at the moment the x-ray was taken. When their consciousness changed, so did the x-ray.

If you are the only subject of a prophesy, you have a great deal of power over whether or not the prediction will manifest itself in your experience. If the photo includes another person, their consciousness and free will contribute to whether or not the prophecy will come about. If a large group of people is involved, such as all the citizens of a country, there are many factors that will determine the outcome. This is why predictions of election results are often wrong; many people are exerting their free will, which can change. Prophecies serve as a good litmus test of where things stand or where they are headed, but they are less reliable as indicators of what will be.

Sorry, We're Out of Time

Guide Mary stated that the guides' other weakness is time. "In our world, time does not exist. So when we see something happening in the world of time, we have difficulty saying when that will occur. To us, past, present, and future all occur simultaneously."

While swimming in the ocean one day, I cut my foot on some coral. I ended up having to favor the foot and keep the wound clean and bandaged. During that time I had a telephone reading with Mary. "If you go swimming, be careful to guard your foot," she told me.

I was astounded—that injury had already occurred. Yet Mary was giving me advice as if the incident had not yet happened. This underscores that the guides have difficulty assessing when an event occurs in time.

The timing of an event also depends on the intention of an individual and the confluence of intentions of everyone involved. The more people involved, the less fixed in time the prophesied event. In 1956 Jean Dixon predicted that the next President would be assassinated during his second term. John F. Kennedy was assassinated toward the end of his first term. So she correctly predicted the event, but the timing was slightly off. Psychics are more in touch with a stream of likely events rather than details.

Choose Your Fortune

Many people give their power away to fortune tellers and depend on their advice to make decisions. Some people fear to make a move until the stars line up in their favor. Others run to mountaintops because they have been told that the world will come to an end when a particular comet passes through the sky. In such cases those seeking guidance are disempowered. To depend on an external source to tell you what to do weakens an individual. Like the sons of the farmer who gained a great boon by cultivating their fields, we advance more through making decisions than through allowing someone to make them for us.

After having lunch with a friend at a Chinese restaurant, the waitress delivered two fortune cookies to our table. When I read my fortune, I found it to be rather bland. I turned to my friend and asked her, "Do you like your fortune?"

"Not especially," she answered, shrugging her shoulders.

I called the waitress.

"Yes, sir?"

"We don't care for the fortunes we've received," I told her. "Would you please bring us some more?"

A minute later our waitress returned with *a whole bowl* of fortune cookies and a smile. She set the bowl on the table and offered, "Take your pick." So we went through the bowl, unraveling fortunes until we each found one we liked.

We can either accept the fortune given to us by others, or we can generate the one we choose. If you feel stuck with the fortune someone has placed before you, you are limiting yourself to the bland fortune cookie. Meanwhile there is a whole bowl available, if you are willing to summon it and live it.

The best way to predict the future is to create it.
—Peter Drucker

HOW TO LEARN FROM
AN IMPURE TEACHER

Abraham underscores the importance of extracting spiritual insights from all of our experiences. The Law of Attraction brings to us the people and events who match the consciousness we are holding. If those encounters are joyful, we have confirmation that we are living in alignment with our true self. If those encounters are painful, we have stepped out of alignment, and we are being called to make a vital course correction.

A Course in Miracles tells us, "All things are lessons God would have me learn." We grow through happy, rewarding experiences, as well as painful ones. If we learn from a poor decision, it becomes our friend. So even bad decisions are good ones in progress. We also learn from observing the decisions others make, and the results they accrue. Everyone is our teacher. Some teach us what to do, and others teach us what not to do.

In the illuminating documentary *Kumare*, an American fellow of Indian heritage conducts an experiment in which he passes himself off as a guru to see who will follow him and how his instruction affects their lives. He takes a phony Hindu name, puts on a thick accent, sets up yoga, meditation, and eastern philosophy classes, and conducts personal coaching sessions. Soon he attracts a dedicated coterie of students who follow his teachings religiously. As a result of their faith in the guru and their dedicated practices, they become healthier, happier, and more prosperous, their relationships improve, and they experience significant quality-of-life upgrades—even while their teacher was a fake. The positive effects were a result more of the teachings than the teacher, the disciples' application more than the guru's qualifications. Yoga, meditation, and spiritual principles work if you put them into action—even if the teacher does not practice them himself. In the process, Kumare himself experienced a profound transformation. So, you can learn from an unqualified teacher. But, of course, you will do better to find a qualified one.

Charlatans or misguided teachers provide us with some of the best lessons on our spiritual path. If you have been influenced or duped by a less-than-qualified teacher, do not dub yourself a victim or write the experience off as a waste of time. Used wisely, it can become one of the most valuable educations of your life.

A student came to Hilda Charlton and complained that he had been ripped off by an auto mechanic. "When I took my car to this guy, I had a bad feeling about him. But he seemed to know what he was doing, so I hired him to fix the car for $500," the student explained. "When I got the car back, it still didn't work. I took it back to him and he still couldn't fix it. I lost all that money in the deal."

Hilda replied, "Imagine that I offered a weekly course on how to get in touch with your intuition so you will make effective decisions and never be duped. Let's say the seminar tuition was $500 and I guaranteed that you would get so connected with your inner guidance that you would make wiser decisions for the rest of your life. Would that course be worth the tuition for you?"

"Absolutely!" the student replied.

"Then be glad you just received all the benefits of such a course without having to attend the whole seminar," Hilda explained. "The auto mechanic was your teacher. The next time something does not feel right, will you listen to your intuition?"

"You bet!"

"Then the money you invested was the price of your education. Bless the experience as a huge accelerator of your growth, and move on."

Take the Best and Leave the Rest

Even bad teachers utter some nuggets of truth that can change your life if you put them into action. ("Even a clock that is stopped is right twice a day.") If you focus on the truth and not the falsehoods, you can advance not because of the teacher, but because universal principles work, no matter who utters them, or who does or doesn't practice them. They work because you apply them.

The clever film *The Man Who Knew Too Little* introduces us to a naïve fellow who is invited to participate in a murder mystery party. Due to a strange twist of events, he gets involved in a real murder plot, and the villains attempt to kill him. But because he thinks the adverse events are just a big game, he has no fear and he dances through them playfully, thwarting the killers at every turn. Ultimately, his naïveté serves as an asset. In this case, what he didn't know didn't hurt him, but significantly helped him. His positive consciousness protected him from those with sullied intentions.

If we threw out all teachers who make mistakes or spout untruths, there would be no teachers left. We do better to take the best and leave the rest. What a tragic loss it would be to discount or deny the blessings imperfect teachers deliver because they make some mistakes. Every teaching has its place, including erroneous ones that motivate you to find the truth they overlooked. Manure smells bad but it serves as excellent fertilizer if you know where to put it.

Like all of us, channelers, psychics, and healers have their own human journey, karma, and learning curve. Just because a channel struggles with personal dilemmas does not disqualify their channeling. It just means that they are facing lessons they need to master.

If a channel can sufficiently detach from his personality while in the channeling state, he can still bring through sublime, divine teachings. The channel is simply delivering the teachings, not sourcing them. Don't confuse the message with the messenger. All true teachings come from God. If teachings are right for you, God will get them to you, sometimes through unlikely or imperfect avenues.

Ultimately all illusions, including falsehoods spouted by an impure teacher, are exposed and the truth they concealed is revealed. Such truths come even more powerfully because the contrast that led us to them is sharp. Both the good and the bad are elements in your education. If you know how to work wisely with the bad, it becomes good. Seen from an expanded perspective, the negative contributes to the positive.

I am not suggesting you stay with a teacher who is seriously dysfunctional or abusive. If the cons far outweigh the pros, it is time to move on. In such a case the lesson may be for you to sharpen your discernment, set healthy boundaries, and leave. Yet leave not with anger or resentment, but with gratitude for the insights you gained in staying, and the strength you gained in leaving.

From Hype to Healing

Many years ago a group of my friends were flocking to a spiritual teacher who was reported to have terrific psychic powers and a direct connection to God. Several teachers I highly respected declared this teacher an enlightened being. Titillated, I wanted to receive the gifts from such a rare soul.

I attended one of the teacher's classes, but I did not feel anything special. The woman was clever and entertaining, yet when I left the class I felt flat and uninspired. Yet my friends who attended with me were buzzing with excitement, touting her praises. I figured there must be something wrong with me, some resistance that was keeping me from recognizing the value of her teachings. So I went to another class.

During that class the teacher called on me and we had a one-to-one conversation. Then she invited me to attend her special series of classes for advanced students. I was flattered, and accepted.

I went to those classes for six months, at significant effort. The scene was entwined with intrigue, drama, gossip, and mystery. The location of the classes moved from day to day; I never knew where we would meet until the night before the class. I would receive a phone call at 3:00 a.m. with cryptic instructions about how to find tomorrow morning's meeting at a remote secret location four hours from my home. Not wanting to miss a meeting, my life began to revolve around attending these classes.

Yet if I were honest, I would have admitted that I was not receiving much spiritual value from this teacher or her classes. I was more drawn to follow the crowd, and revel in the pride of being in this master's inner circle. My actions were devoted, but my heart was empty.

Then the shift hit the fan. One of the teacher's top students exposed her to be a hypocrite and a fraud. While she required her students to be celibate, she was having sex with one of them. While she prescribed strict rituals, she made fun of them in private. And on and on. As more revelations came forth, her organization fell apart. While some dedicated students remained, most headed for the hills, along with me.

Looking back, I recognized that it was not my spiritual guidance that moved me to follow this leader, but my ego. I had gotten caught up in the hype, fearing I would miss out on something valuable, and I succumbed to pride about being in her inner circle—all the wrong reasons for following a teacher or teaching.

Yet the lesson I gleaned made the experience golden. Never again would I override my intuition. I would follow teachings only if they resonated with my soul. I would not give my power to the opinions of others; instead, I would trust my deep inner knowing. Over the many years since that experience occurred, it has proven to be one of the most valuable on my spiritual journey. I now know with powerful confidence that we all have a sterling inner compass that guides us to discern between what matches our well-being and what does not.

You and I are immersed in the highest education possible—the awakening of our soul. While you may have been attracted to a teacher for the lessons you expected, there were deeper, more subtle learnings to be gained. Jewish theologian Martin Buber said, "All journeys have secret destinations of which the traveler is unaware." You thought you were doing something for one reason, but God had a bigger idea. When we recognize and appreciate that idea, our journey makes sense and we recognize that every step has taken us closer to home, including the apparent detours.

DIRECT CONNECT 24
Reframing Impure Teachers

Have you ever studied with a teacher, psychic, or healer who gave you misleading information or turned out to be a phony?

How did you react to discovering the deficit in the teacher or teaching?

What beliefs within you (1) attracted a person who deceived you, and (2) allowed you to stay with that person?

What did you learn from the experience?

Would you be as likely to attract someone of compromised integrity again or participate in such a scenario?

If there were positive elements of your relationship with the teacher and the teachings, what good can you take from the experience?

What unwanted elements would you like to leave behind?

How did this experience ultimately benefit you?

THE GURU IN YOU

Abraham is a huge proponent of self-reliance—not the small, fearful, defensive, limited self, but the grand Self that resides at the core of our being. Abraham would not have you look up to another personage, except for inspiration as a role model. Instead, look within for the part of you connected to pure Source energy. The only person to become is yourself.

As composer George Gershwin's career was rising, he contacted his role model Maurice Ravel and asked if Ravel would take him on as a student. Ravel, familiar with Gershwin's work, rejected him, replying, "Why become a second-rate Ravel when you are already a first-rate Gershwin?"

A true teacher does not lead students to imitate the teacher, but instead inspires students to bring forth their own greatness. Such a mentor makes himself progressively more unnecessary. Certainly we can learn from experts and benefit from emulating their model. What we do with the model carves the difference between a student who mimics a master and one who becomes a master.

When I was in graduate school studying to become a human relations trainer, my professor said, *"A consultant is someone who borrows your watch to tell you what time it is."* This was an especially bold missive from a teacher who was training us to be consultants! If you don't know how to tell time and you need to know the time now, a consultant is a wise investment. But if you can learn to tell time yourself, you will save lots of money and hassles in the long run.

A friend of mine was studying with a shaman in New Mexico. She asked him, "How can I be more like you?" He replied, "The way to be more like me is to be more like you." The message was that the shaman's talents sprang from allowing his true self to shine. The student's talents would spring from her allowing *her* true self to shine.

Ralph Waldo Emerson said, "Imitation is suicide." You can follow in someone else's footsteps for a while, but then you must impress your own footprints. My mentor stated, "The student should seek to devour the teacher." A good student strives not just to learn from the teacher or equal her, but to surpass the teacher. To simply replicate a teacher's method or material fails to fulfill the highest potential of the teacher-student relationship. Every generation should stand on the shoulders of the previous one. I am excited when my students come up with ideas, techniques, or successes beyond what I have taught them. I encourage them to carry the torch into their own domain and add their own flair to it. I am not diminished by my students' triumphs. I am honored by them.

Your Teacher Is an Aspect of Yourself

I have heard students ask channelers, "Is [Name of Entity] really speaking through you, or are you simply accessing an aspect of your higher mind?" The answer is: both. In the manifest universe there are discreet entities in service to humanity. We don't doubt that we are relating to other people on the physical plane. Why would it be different on the spiritual plane? Bodies are vehicles through which Spirit expresses. Channeled guides are simply people, or streams of wisdom, without bodies. If we are spiritual beings more than physical, why do we give so much power to what a body is doing? It is what the spirit is doing that matters.

Everyone we meet in the apparent outer world, physical and nonphysical, is an aspect or projection of our mind. Beyond the illusion of separate selves, there is one self. Thus a channeled entity is an aspect of the channeler's mind and the minds of all who are aware of the entity. All we ever see is the projection of our own thoughts. But since we believe in separate identities, we prefer to relate to the guide as a unique individual. This works because we believe it. One day we will take back all of our projections and claim the unity we all share.

Spend less time trying to figure out what is the entity's relationship with the channeler, and more time figuring out how the entity represents an aspect of your own psyche. A channeled entity is a disowned part of yourself. You do not accept your innate wisdom, divinity, or higher self, so you see it outside yourself rather than within you. Bashar tells many students, "When you talk to me, you are having a conversation with your own higher mind."

Ultimately, we talk only to ourselves. One day all separate bodies, personalities, teachers, discarnate spirits, and channeled entities will dissolve into the light and there will be only one of us. The play of light and shadows makes it seem that there are separate entities interacting. Every encounter takes us deeper down the rabbit hole of separateness or higher into healing; farther from our true self or closer to it. Evaluate all psychics, channelers, mediums, teachers, and healers on the basis of whether they make you aware of your divine nature, or split you from it.

Early on my spiritual path I read a book by Harvey Freeman titled, *God is the Guru*. That title has stayed with me for many years. Every genuine spiritual guide we meet is a voice for God come to penetrate the world of illusion, extricate humanity from suffering, and gather us back into the arms of love. Whether you are a student or a teacher—we are all both— remember that God is the Voice behind all voices.

Remember What's Important

It can be tempting to get into intellectual discussions or arguments about which channeled entity is real and the gossipy details of the channeler's personal life. I have found such forays to be fruitless, and I suggest you don't get involved in distracting mind games. If you are going to discuss channeled teachings, discuss the content and value of the material rather than the channel's personality or channeling technique.

There are a few simple criteria by which to evaluate any channeled or psychic material: Does it work for you? Is it relevant to your life? Does it bring you closer to inner peace, healing, and soul satisfaction? Does it improve your relationships? Does it identify you as an eternal, immortal being? Does it help you live in the world more joyfully and abundantly? All other questions are meaningless. The only purpose of engaging in any channeled material, as a student or channeler, is to improve the quality of your life and that of others. If the teachings liberate and empower you, no matter who speaks them or how, use the material. If the teachings burden you, confuse you, or generate fear, pain, or conflict, discard them. Maybe the material is erroneous, or it belongs to others, or the timing is not right for you. Apply what works for you and release what doesn't. All else is detail and distraction.

Help! My Guru Died

To learn from a gifted teacher in the flesh, or a person channeling a brilliant nonphysical teacher, is one of the greatest blessings of a lifetime. If you have found such a guide, or you will, appreciate the immense gift you have been given. Grace has embraced you. Such a being can accelerate your spiritual evolution and shortcut a great deal of suffering. A guide like this is sent by God.

What do you do when your psychic, guru, medium, or teacher dies or leaves your life? Are you lost, alone, and abandoned? Do you need to run to find a replacement? Or might you be in a better position to connect with your inner teacher rather than leaning on an outer one?

Several of my most esteemed spiritual guides have departed from this world. Hilda Charlton, Carla Gordan, and Pat Rodegast have laid their bodies aside and gone on. In each case when I received news of their passing, I was shocked and saddened. Surely they would live forever, I thought. But the world of form is not kind to bodies. Eventually they all disappear.

Yet when we can find the gift that a departure delivers, it becomes a blessing. *A Course in Miracles* tells us, "All change is helpful." In the case of Carla's passing, I had to connect with Guide Mary's spirit myself without needing Carla's body to channel for me. Because Mary lives more in energy than in flesh, she, like all friends in high places, is available to anyone seeking to contact her. When I realized the invitation before me, I began to tune in to Mary. Eventually I found her. Now when I perceive a problem or I have an important decision to make, I ask Mary and I listen for the answer. A true teacher of God, she always replies. When I tap into her frequency, I have access to all the wisdom she passed along through Carla, and which she continues to offer.

You can connect with any spiritual master, in the physical dimension or elsewhere, by sending forth a request for help. This is no imaginary conversation. All the support you need is available. Simply get quiet and ask sincerely. Your answers will come. What loving God would withhold help from a beloved child?

DIRECT CONNECT 25
Establish Your Own Connection

Do you have a valued mentor who has left your life either by passing on or moving away?

If so, does a part of you wish that person was still available to you?

What does the part of your mind that misses that person say?

What does the part of your mind that accepts your independence say?

Through what means can you still connect with your valued guide?

How has the physical person's departure strengthened you?

What relationship would you now like to develop with your guide?

Running Elsewhere

Some students, upon losing their teacher, grow frantic and lurch with eyes wide shut for a substitute. This rarely works. In such cases, the student is motivated by fear and lack, not soul strength and abundant supply. Desperate actions beget desperate results.

After Carla passed, I felt lost and I fervently wanted to find a medium to replace her. A friend told me about a channeler she thought was quite good, and I went to see her. At first, I was enamored with this teacher and hoped I had found someone to deliver the same quality of teaching that Carla had disseminated. We had a kind of honeymoon relationship. But, like romantic honeymoons, spiritual honeymoons eventually give way to reality. This channeler, although well-intended and gifted in her own way, did not deliver the caliber of teaching I had come to know. She gave me a few accurate and helpful pieces of information, but I had to sift them out from other distracting elements and personality issues. When I realized that I had allowed desperation to be my guide, I withdrew my starry-eyed hope that she would be my next savior. That relationship was analogous to a romantic rebound.

At a later date, a friend casually introduced me to Bashar, who became my valued guide for many years. Bashar's orientation is quite different than Carla's, but excellent and extremely helpful in its own right. I wasn't looking to him for psychic readings, but for soul guidance. I didn't get the form of teaching I was used to, but I got what I needed. Spirit knows your needs better than you do. When you trust Higher Power, everything you need comes to you easily and effortlessly, including the teachers and teachings that will most advance your spiritual and material journeys.

Where the Master Lives

A seminar participant asked me, "How can I let in more love from my girlfriend?" I told him, "It's not your girlfriend's love you need to let in. It's your own love you need to let out."

This fellow's question is analogous to a spiritual seeker asking, "How can I find and learn from a spiritual master?" The answer is: *It's not the external master you need to import. It's the internal master you need to express.* While you may not regard yourself as a spiritual master, you must claim the part of you that knows what you need to know rather than seeking someone outside you to answer your questions.

A Course in Miracles tells us that in any situation in which you perceive something is missing, what is missing is what you are not giving. This statement is highly confrontive, even insulting to the ego, which swears that if something in your life is missing, it is because someone or something out there is withholding. Our pain or sense of lack always seems to be someone else's fault: My husband doesn't share my spiritual path; my parents don't validate me; my ex doesn't raise our kids properly; my company doesn't pay me enough; my family won't allow me to marry the person I am in love with. Our emptiness never has anything to do with our own consciousness, ego argues; we are innocent victims.

This dynamic also creeps into spiritual paths and religions that teach you to draw energy from your mentor, guru, or savior. If you absorb positive healing energy, you will be healed. So you sit quietly and open yourself to take in the chi, prana, mana, shakti, orgone energy, or whatever you name it. Then you feel better and thank the guru for healing you.

This technique surely works, and if this is your spiritual practice, I encourage you to continue. Any method that achieves healing is valid, and should be used diligently. All healing is of God, regardless of the channel through with it comes. If you are benefitting from drawing energy from an external source, you are being blessed.

Yet eventually you must consider whether the healing energy is coming from outside you or from within you. Is your guru or savior really a separate entity who transmits healing, or does he or she live within you? Could your spiritual master actually be an aspect of your own higher self? Thus you are not reaching out for your answer, but tapping in.

Ram Dass's guru Maharaj-ji told him, "Guru, God, and Self are one." This is the meditation of a lifetime! The guru and God we strive to reach out there are really our own Self. We make up stories of division and then struggle to bridge a gap that doesn't exist. Rather than seeking a guru to save you, seek to dissolve the false sense of separation that tells you that the guru lives in a distant city or time rather than in your own heart now. The guru is not is a separate entity, but your true Christed self.

Your inner teacher is the realest part of your mind. The outer teacher is your "permission slip" to remind you what you already know. Keep using that permission slip as long as it works; it is a blessing from God. Yet the greatest blessing is to recognize that God and all good dwell within you, as you. Then you won't need to let in more love from your partner or the world. You will already own all the love you could ever need.

After we have consulted with psychics, studied with channelers, meditated, prayed, and done all of our spiritual practices, we discover that the one we have been searching for lives in our own heart. Thus we move from mystery to mastery. The wisdom we hunger for was within us all the time. No matter how many mountains we climb, oceans we cross, and gurus we bow before, we eventually realize that we carried our home with us all along. Let us hasten there now.

DIRECT CONNECT 26

The Answer Lies Within

What question would you like a psychic, channeler, medium, or teacher to answer for you?

If you could get that answer from your own divine inner knowing, would you reach for it and accept it?

Take a few moments now to close your eyes, take some deep breaths, get quiet, and drop in the depths of your own heart. If it helps to visualize your guru or mentor, do so. Then ask your question and listen for your answer. What do you hear?

When you feel complete, write down your answer. From time to time, revisit it, meditate on it, and ask your Higher Self if It would like to add anything to it, or what is your message for the current moment.

I have chosen to introduce you to these entities and channelers because none of them foster students' dependence on them. They all guide students to find answers within their own heart. They honor the God in the students and do not seek to make gods of themselves. They serve an interim function, and encourage students to channel their own divine selves.

Lesson 189 of *A Course in Miracles* advises students to "Be still, and lay aside all thoughts of what you are and what God is . . . Forget this world, forget this course, and come with wholly empty hands unto your God." The highest teachings urge you to go beyond them. Valuable trainings have a graduation mechanism; they don't cast you as a student for a lifetime or forever. Instead, they empower you to put the training behind you, and become one with your Source. Rather than worshipping God, you become an expression of God.

PART VII

BASHAR:

SHARING A
GREATER UNIVERSE

REALITY BY CHOICE

When Darryl Anka experienced a close UFO sighting, he had no idea how that encounter would change his life and the lives of many thousands to follow. While driving with some friends in Los Angeles in broad daylight, Darryl noticed an unusual object hovering about 150 feet away from him. "The craft was triangular in form, each side about thirty feet in length, fabricated of a dark metallic substance," he recounts. The ship hovered for a few minutes and then disappeared.   Several days later another craft, identical in size and construction, appeared to Darryl, this time at a distance of sixty feet. On both occasions Darryl's companions concurred with the sighting.

As a result of these encounters, Darryl became intensely interested in UFO's and metaphysics. He dove into their study with zeal, seeking to gain as much knowledge as possible about those realms. He signed up for a course in channeling, not to become a channel, but to understand how the phenomenon works.

During that course, Darryl received a telepathic communication from a being who identified himself as an extraterrestrial from the future. The entity's purpose, it explained, is to guide us in our spiritual and technological advancement and prepare the way for open contact with civilizations from beyond Earth. The entity identified himself as "Bashar," adding that spiritual beings do not use names as we call each other—they are instead recognizable by their unique frequency. Such beings choose names only to enable human beings to relate to them. Considering that Darryl has some Arabic ancestry, the entity chose a name that in that language means "messenger."

Following the Signs

I was introduced to Bashar by Peter Beamish, the filmmaker of Abraham-Hicks' video *The Secret Behind the Secret.* I wrote to Peter when I was seeking guidance about making a movie of my metaphysical novel, *Linden's Last Life.* After our business discussion, Peter suggested, "You might want to check out a channeled entity named Bashar. He has some good things to say."

I searched YouTube and found a video in which Bashar was explaining the dynamics behind teleportation. At first, I was leery. Darryl, channeling Bashar, sat onstage between two large crystals, each glowing with shifting colors from a revolving light. *Oh, so new-agey.* Darryl wore a Hawaiian shirt, jeans, and sneakers. While I am a fan of Hawaiian shirts, his presentation seemed unduly casual.

Yet as I listened to Bashar's talk, I was impressed. Bashar gave a detailed technical explanation of how teleportation can be achieved, using a foundation of advanced physics. While I am not a scientist, the dynamics seemed quite plausible, simplified so a lay person could grasp the technique and its potential for humanity. Bashar delivered his explanation with impressive authority and detail.

My skepticism dissolving, I began to explore more of Bashar's YouTube presentations. He covered a vast range of topics: parallel realities; interstellar travel; the untold origin of humanity; relationships; reincarnation; angels; death; meditation; physical healing; abundance; the future of the human race; and other fascinating explorations. The more I heard, the more I recognized that, whoever this source was, it was tapped into a vast reservoir of lofty yet practical wisdom. I was not only being educated but inspired and entertained. While communicating in a bold, direct manner, Bashar was also quite funny, and could be soft and cuddly when appropriate.

Darryl Anka has been channeling Bashar since 1981, generating a substantial body of work. Bashar is a bit unusual in the realm of channeled entities in that he maintains that he is not simply a discarnate entity speaking through a living person, but he also has a physical life during a time period approximately 2700 years in our future. Bashar identifies himself as an aspect of the future self of Darryl, come to complete a soul contract that Darryl made with him for service to humanity.

Parallel Realities

Earlier I mentioned that we live in a universe of many simultaneous parallel realities. Bashar explains that when you make a change in your life, or seek to make a change in the world, you are not altering the reality you are coming from. Instead, you are entering a new reality matching the one you desire.

My friend Tina had been dating a fellow named Chris for a while, in hopes of establishing a long-term relationship. But eventually she realized that Chris was not ready for such a commitment, and she broke up with him. She told her friends, "I refuse to see unavailable men anymore."

One day several months later, Tina was shopping in a mall with her pre-teen son, when the boy began to tug on her sleeve. "Why aren't you answering Chris?" he asked. Confused, Tina asked the boy what he was talking about.

"Chris has been standing a few feet from you for a couple minutes, trying to get your attention, but you've been ignoring him," the boy explained.

Tina looked up and, sure enough, there was Chris standing before her. He had coincidentally been in the same store, noticed Tina, and came over to say hello. But she did not see or hear him until her son called her attention to him.

Tina later told me, "When I said, 'I refuse to see unavailable men anymore,' the universe took me literally!'"

Like Tina, we all see the world that matches our desires, choices, and intentions, and worlds that have nothing to do with our thoughts and energy remain invisible to us. But all the worlds are there. We just see the one equivalent to the consciousness we are holding.

How, then, do you shift to a parallel reality that matches your values and intentions? Focus on everything about that reality that you value. Think, feel, know, talk, and live it. When you are immersed in your vision, the Law of Attraction will draw to you the perfect people and events to match your intention. If you are busy focusing on what is not working or the reality you are trying to get away from, you stay stuck in those conditions. Mind is creative, no matter where you point it. "This is simply physics," Bashar explains. "It's just how the universe operates."

> ## DIRECT CONNECT 27
> ### Navigating Parallel Realities
>
> Have you ever found yourself in a reality discontinuous with the reality you usually experience? If so, describe that alternate reality:
>
> How do you think you stepped into that experience?
>
> If you could create or live in an alternative reality preferable to the one you usually experience, what would that reality be?
>
> What might you do to facilitate entering your preferred reality?

A Broader View of Reincarnation

Bashar tells that our commonly-held understanding of reincarnation is somewhat simplistic and limited. It bears working value, but requires a broader view to be truly grasped. We do not live many different lives sequentially in time, as many people believe. More precisely, we are living all of those lives simultaneously. This idea boggles the intellect because we are accustomed to thinking in terms of linear time in which one thing happens after another. But, as spiritual beings, we are not subject to the trappings of time. Remove time from the equation, and it's all happening now. I love novelist Ray Cummings' description that "time is what keeps everything from happening at once."

When you connect with a "past life," you are actually connecting with another life that exists right beside this one. So, you are not going back in time. You are just moving your point of attention to another location on the universal matrix. You could just as easily connect to a future life. *Déjà vu* is a kind of bleed-through in which you know what is happening before it happens because it has *already* happened and you are remembering it.

Taking this concept deeper, you do not have certain fixed past lives. When you connect to a specific past life, you are tapping into one that matches your current state of consciousness. Tomorrow you could have a different past life because that one is more connected to who you are at the time you are checking in.

This explains why so many people simultaneously believe they were Cleopatra, Joan of Arc, Napoleon, or any other historical figure. While lots of these speculations may be simply wishful thinking, in some sense they may be true in that the individual is at the moment tapped into the consciousness of that figure, and has achieved vibrational resonance with him. Let's say that you sense that you or someone you know was St. Francis in a past life. But St. Francis was not simply a monk who loved nature and talked to animals. He was—and is—a vast and powerful spirit that extends far beyond the body that walked the hills of Assisi for four short decades 800 years ago. That was just one body and personality that focalized a far grander self and brought it to Earth to manifest the good that he did. The vibrant soul of St. Francis lives *now* as much as ever. Think of St. Francis more as a state of consciousness than as a person. When you align with his energy, you open the door to experience his presence in your life, walk the path he walked, and uplift our world today.

This model explains how Jesus or any spiritual master can simultaneously achieve many apparitions, conversations, healings, and manifestations. Such advanced beings can be in many places at once because spirit is not tied to location any more than it is bound by time. Thus millions of people can speak with Jesus and receive his blessing at the same moment. Some yogis have demonstrated bilocation, where they physically show up in different places at the same time. Neem Karoli Baba and Satya Sai Baba, for example, have been documented to physically be in several different locations at once. Bashar explains that once again this is a simple application of higher physics.

Let's take this sublime dynamic to the ultimate level: You are not simply one person connecting with a past life or a simultaneously occurring one. You are God inhabiting all realities, experiencing an infinite number of lives. God is the love and intelligence that fills all time and space—actually far *beyond* time and space—poking Its head through a myriad of holes to observe and experience life from countless perspectives. As one philosopher stated, "God is a flower that grew a nose to smell itself."

You can also think of God as a vast hand fitting itself into a glove with an infinite number of fingers. When life force (another name for God) slips into a particular glove finger—which we call a "body"—that glove finger moves and appears to have a reality of its own. But the glove is actually inert, with no life or power of its own. All of its movement derives from the unseen finger animating it. When God removes the finger from the glove, that body wilts and can live no more. We call this "death." Yet the energy that enlivened the body still exists, in the myriad of glove fingers still animated, and beyond them. So death is just the shifting of life force from one expression to another.

Ultimately you are God living through everyone and everything that has ever lived, is living, or will live. You are also God without any form at all. God does not depend on things. Things depend on God. When we identify with one body or personality, we are shrinking the allness of God to a very small and limited container. That contraction serves a purpose for specific learning and service in the world. But ultimately, we cannot maintain happiness being a body only. The awareness of our higher, vaster, realer self is the goal we all strive for. All of our human seeking leads us to divine seeking, which leads to divine finding. Eventually we tire of being a tiny speck and we yearn to be all. The day comes when allness becomes more appealing than smallness. At that point, life becomes new and it takes on infinitely more glorious meaning.

DIRECT CONNECT 28
Past Lives or Simultaneous?

Do you believe you have lived one or more lifetimes before this one? If so, who were you?

Is it possible that what appears to be previous lifetimes are all occurring simultaneously?

How have you or other people used the idea of reincarnation in a way that accelerates your spiritual growth?

How have you or other people used the idea of reincarnation to distract you from your spiritual growth or impede it?

If you are God showing up as you to explore and experience the world from a unique perspective, how would you describe that perspective?

How does your unique perspective contribute to your life and the world?

Credit Where Credit Is Due

One aspect of Bashar's teaching that I most respect is his unwillingness to claim credit or responsibility for what his students receive through his teachings. In all cases he acknowledges the students for creating their own experience—which serves as a sublime education in itself.

"Thank you for helping me to see a greater truth," a student states. "Thank you for being willing to see a greater truth," Bashar replies. "My heart is open now that I have interacted with you," the next student acknowledges. "That's because you chose to open your heart." "I feel freer than I have in a long time," says another. Bashar answers, "You were ready for freedom and you claimed it."

Such unwavering empowerment of the student draws a crucial line between teachers who seek to cultivate independent students, and teachers who seek to keep students dependent on the teacher. It is a rare teacher who deflects responsibility for the students' progress and identifies it squarely as the students' choice. Beware of any teacher who claims that he or she is doing it *for* you. Real teachers revel in students becoming free of the need for a teacher. You can assess the integrity and maturity of a teacher by how much he or she empowers the student rather than entrapping the student in a false sense of need or reliance on the teacher. A teacher who does things for the student that she can do for herself is robbing the student of a muscle she could build that will empower her for a lifetime.

Authentic teachers identify Spirit as the power behind all manifestations. Jesus stated clearly, "It is not I, but the Father within me Who does the work." When people called Jesus "rabbi" (teacher), he affirmed, "You have but one teacher—your heavenly Father." If Jesus claimed no credit for his great works, and honored Higher Power as his Source, then you and I must also give credit where credit is due.

DIRECT CONNECT 29
Who Deserves Credit?

If you are studying with a mentor or healer, does that person claim credit for their students' healing or success, or do they credit the students?

If you are serving as a teacher, healer, or therapist, do you claim credit for your clients' healing or success, or do you credit the clients and God through the clients?

How, as a student, can you accept more responsibility for your experience?

How, as a teacher, can you empower your students to recognize that they are the source of their experience?

The Sword of Truth

Bashar is bold, honest, and incisive with his students, and does not hesitate to tell them what they need to know to advance on their path. Such loving confrontation challenges Bashar's students, as it pokes holes in faulty belief systems and calls them to come out from hiding. A worthy spiritual teacher does not withhold information that can help a student grow, even if the student's ego resists. A spiritual master uses a sharp sword of truth to slice away illusions. Archangel Michael is often depicted as holding a gleaming sword, which represents the blade of truth that vanquishes fear and negation in order to release the authentic self into full expression.

I have also seen Bashar treat students with extraordinary gentleness, softness, and patience. He alters his approach depending on what the student needs. Armored students need their defense system to be penetrated. More fragile students need bolstering and validation. A good teacher tailors his approach to what will most serve the student's temperament. Hilda Charlton said that every person has veered from God either through arrogance or unworthiness. The arrogant need to be cut down and the unworthy need to be empowered. Sincere students love and thank Bashar, even if his communication with them is intense. They recognize his pure intention to help them.

I have had several personal coaching sessions with Bashar, in which I have seen him shift his approach to accommodate what I need. In one session he consistently confronted me and called my ego's bluff. I loved the interaction! I felt no ego, venom, or attack from him. All I sensed was love, support, and impeccable intention. In another session he was soothing and comforting. At another time Bashar told me to get firmer on my decisions and act on them more quickly and sharply. I told Bashar, "I always come to you with lots of questions that I think will take far longer than an hour for you to answer. Then you nail them quickly and we have time left over." He replied, "I don't need to beat around the bush, and neither do you." A world-class teaching in one short statement!

THE CONTACT SPECIALIST

Bashar claims that he is a descendant of his civilization's lineage of "first contact specialists." Such individuals reach out to civilizations like Earth that have arrived at a state of evolution where they are ready to accept and interact with galactic neighbors. These specialists find ways to reach people who are open to contact, educate them, plant a vision of what to expect when contact is made, and help them feel comfortable with the process. When a student asked Bashar, "Why don't you just land a spaceship on the White House lawn?" he asked in turn, "Would you dive into the middle of a group of crazy people with guns?"

The 1951 classic sci-fi film *The Day the Earth Stood Still* provides an accurate representation of how interstellar visitors would likely be treated with fear, defensiveness, and violence rather than receptivity and a sense of mutual exploration. While governments may represent the majority of their citizens, they generally do not represent the element of humanity on the leading edge of conscious evolution on the planet. In *The Day the Earth Stood Still*, the visiting extraterrestrial did not contact the government. Instead, he reached out to a coterie of open-minded forward thinkers. I often quote President Eisenhower's brilliant prediction:

"I think that people want peace so much that one of these days government had better get out of their way and let them have it."

The notion that we earthlings are the only intelligent beings in the physical universe is an egotistical assumption of gargantuan proportion. Even hard-core scientists admit that the number of galaxies, stars, and planets in the known universe, let alone the unknown universe, is so vast that we cannot be the only kids on the block. Add to the mix the existence of nonphysical dimensions, and it becomes obvious that we share creation with a myriad of other living beings. One survey revealed that the number of people who believe in extraterrestrials is greater than the number who believe that their social security benefits will be available when they are ready for them. Some surveys indicate that more than half of the population believes that extraterrestrials have visited Earth. If contact specialists are reaching out to us, we may be more ready than ever to receive them.

Why Are They Here?

Lots of folks speculate on why extraterrestrials would come to our world and interact with us. Some postulate that aliens are here to help us, while others fear they are here to enslave or annihilate us. Bashar states that there are two basic reasons for E.T.s' presence here:

First, they are here to assist us in our spiritual and technological evolution. Bashar states that his civilization, known as "Sessani," are ahead of our development by over two millennia. The Sessani have evolved to the point where they are quasi-physical, fully telepathic, and live by divinely orchestrated synchronicity. They do not eat or sleep, and they reproduce energetically with their minds. The Sessani are gentle and pacifistic, seeking to be of service where they can. Bashar's teachings have assisted many thousands of people in our world to grow spiritually. If his influence as an individual is any indication of what the Sessani can do as a race, we have benevolent elder siblings reaching out to help us grow.

Advanced cultures can also introduce us to technologies that can enhance our well-being. Bashar has answered numerous questions related to physical healing, free energy, traveling beyond light speed, and more. While he sometimes delivers specific formulas and blueprints, more often he offers paradigms and hints, indicating that we must participate in the technologies' development so we understand it and can master it. We must do our homework.

The second reason extraterrestrials approach Earth is to protect themselves. The wave of UFO encounters began soon after World War II, when the United States dropped two atomic bombs on Japan and detonated many test devices before and after that pivotal event. Since that time, numerous other nations have developed nuclear weaponry. Such explosions, Bashar explains, negatively impact our cosmic neighbors by warping the fabric of time and space. This process disturbs the aliens' ability to safely maneuver their craft, along with other destructive results. For this reason, our E.T. friends have been monitoring and policing us to prevent us from initiating atomic warfare. There are many documented cases in which U.S. and other nations' nuclear silos have been totally disabled immediately after military personnel observed unidentifiable craft over the base. (For a fascinating overview of these and related incidents, read *UFOs: Generals, Pilots and Government Officials Go on the Record* by respected veteran journalist Leslie Kean.) The message behind these interventions is that if any nation attempts to start a nuclear war, those weapons would be deactivated before they could launch. This is the one scenario in which extraterrestrial visitors would be permitted to violate the Prime Directive to not interfere with a developing civilization, which Bashar confirms is a very real edict in interplanetary relations.

Bashar also acknowledges that there are some alien visitors with less than benevolent agendas. The dark side has its influence. He assures us, however, that we are capable to choose a reality in which those forces remain in their sector and we advance independent of their intentions.

Aspects of Us

I have stated many times that what appears to be the external world is but a screen upon which we project our beliefs. Extraterrestrial phenomena are no exception. Everything we see "out there" represents a thought we hold in mind. Whether you see sweet childlike intergalactic visitors emerging from a *Close Encounters* mothership, or aggressive Klingons activating a death ray to obliterate humanity, everything you observe is a mirror of your psyche.

Extraterrestrial visitation provides us with an exquisite celestial ink-blot projective test of our beliefs as individuals and humanity as a whole. Fear shows us threat, invasion, and destruction. Love shows us security, connection, and expansion. If you are afraid of an alien invasion, you have a golden opportunity to probe your mind to discover and heal limiting beliefs. Do you believe you are vulnerable? Powerless? Are there bullies on the block that seek to harass and injure you? Are you incapable of protecting yourself? Is the vast unknown a dangerous place where evil lurks and monsters can leap out of the dark to devour you?

Or, by contrast, do you believe that the universe is in the hands of a Higher Power that supports our well-being?

Are we protected by our nature as spiritual beings, the off-spring of a loving, omnipotent God? Are there intelligent beings out there who wish to help us, can, and will? Are there advanced life forms, evolved far beyond us, that would not hurt us even if they could? Is deep space a hiding place for the devil, or is it a field of unlimited opportunities?

Whether or not aliens visit us or reveal themselves, the above inquiries are the ones that will pave our way to richer quality of life on Earth. Ultimately the answers we seek will not be found on this planet or others. The physical plane is a very slim slice of reality, quite deceptive in its depiction of what is available. We will never find a permanent home on Earth because we are not from the Earth. *We* are the extra-terrestrials, which means, "beyond Earth." Our true nature belongs to a higher reality. Our souls will never be satisfied in three or four dimensions. We are all just visiting this planet.

Our intrigue with flying saucers and alien visitors is a form of searching for our higher selves. A part of us senses that there must be more than our earthly existence offers; eventually every soul realizes "this can't be it." So we look skyward for salvation rather than looking soulward. It seems easier to research the Face on Mars than to look in the mirror at our own face. It is more attractive to plan to migrate to a sister Earth rather than face and solve our problems on this one. Truth be told, if we found another planet to live on without cleaning up this one, it would be only a matter of time before the next landing place would replicate pollution and corruption. Taking our current consciousness with us would simply recreate our current problems. What's the use of communicating with interstellar beings when you can't communicate with your husband or wife or children or boss or neighbors? Why build schools on the moon when children on Earth have to pass through metal detectors to get to their classrooms? Why expect to peacefully colonize Venus when so many nations on Earth are at war? We won't be rescued from our earthly dilemmas like the seniors on the boat beamed up into the heavens in the movie *Cocoon*. That vision is a metaphor for elevating our consciousness above limited worldly thinking. Our goal is not to run away from Earth, but to graduate from it by mastering the lessons it offers. We will not escape from suffering by a geographical move; only spiritual advancement will free us.

In the brilliant movie *Contact,* an extraterrestrial civilization sends messages guiding the people of Earth to build a device that will hurtle a human being into the far reaches of outer space. Scientist Ellie Hathaway signs up for the ride; when the machine is activated, she blasts off on a spectacular journey where she travels to a far-distant paradise-like planet and meets a gentle benevolent alien. For the sake of Ellie's comfort, the guide takes the form of her beloved father who died when she was a child. Ellie is ecstatic to reunite with her dad and then to receive wisdom from a spiritual being advanced millions of years beyond our own civilization. When she returns to Earth, Ellie learns that the spaceship in which she sat went nowhere. The entire experience occurred within her mind.

This plot is far closer to truth than fiction. All experiences on Earth and beyond occur within our own psyche. We are not in the world. The world is in us. Visitors from outer space represent higher, more expansive thoughts descending to meet and guide us. Some E.T. aficionados believe that extraterrestrials are angels from God, and all the angel encounters documented in the Bible were actually visitations by aliens. You can see how interchangeable those two belief systems are. Ultimately aliens do not come from Zeta Reticuli. While they might also be physical, they essentially come from your mind. If you like what you see, you have done well. If not, you have your homework to do.

You are the contact specialist that will successfully unite the celestial with the terrestrial. *You* are the bridge between heaven and earth. Through your strides and mine, the day will come when we make open contact with visitors from the stars. That day will be wondrous indeed. The only event more wondrous will be the day we make open contact with ourselves.

DIRECT CONNECT 30

Just Visiting the Planet

Do you believe Earth has been visited by beings from outer space?

If so, what do you believe is their purpose?

Have you ever had a sighting or encounter with a UFO or being of extraterrestrial origin?

Is it possible that extraterrestrials represent aspects of ourselves?

If so, what do you believe they represent?

If extraterrestrials were going to contact us, how do you think they would do it?

Do you believe the people of Earth are ready for open contact with an extraterrestrial civilization? Why or why not?

FEET ON THE GROUND

True spiritual teachers know how to navigate the Earth as well as the heavens. Bashar is as practical as he is etheric. He can talk to students about quantum physics, alternate parallel realities, and the interconnectedness of all incarnations. Moments later he is advising on supplements for a healthy diet, how to deal with a husband who drives too fast, and ways to manifest the funds to travel to meet a long-distance lover. He provides a masterful example of integrating subtle dimensions with denser ones.

I learned this lesson very personally when I was invited to present a week-long workshop at a community dedicated to communicating with departed spirits. While planning the program, I had a hard time working out the details of my agreement with the sponsor. Their representative was not responsive and made errors in the arrangements. Finally we got everything lined up, and I flew to the airport near the event that was scheduled to start the next day.

When I arrived at the airport, the community's representative was not there to meet me as planned. I waited for a while and then phoned their office, an hour's drive from the airport. To my surprise, the person who was supposed to pick me up answered the phone.

"Hi, this is Alan. I'm at the airport."

"Oh, I thought you were coming in tomorrow."

I looked at our paperwork. The date we had agreed on was today.

"Please just go to a hotel and I'll pick you up in the morning."

Disappointed and irked, I took a shuttle bus to the local hotel. As we rambled along, I asked my inner guide, "What's the lesson here?"

The voice answered: *What's the use of communicating with the dead if you can't communicate with the living?*

If you've been on the spiritual path for any length of time, or dealt with folks into supernatural or nonphysical entities, you've probably discovered that a fair amount of such people can be spacey or flaky—some with great confidence. They are so involved with higher dimensions that they lose track of this one. But does it have to be so? Can you navigate paranormal spaces without being spaced out? How do the channelers mentioned in this book function in the world when so much of their attention is pointed skyward? Is it possible to keep your head in the clouds and your feet on the ground? In this chapter we will explore what it takes establish ourselves in a higher dimension and still thrive on Earth.

The Necessity of Higher Perspective

To master the material world, you must rise above it. The physical dimension is a massive constriction of all you are and all that is. If you believe that physical laws and social mores define reality, you will get jammed into one tiny corner of the universe. The recognition that there is more to life than physical eyes can see gives you huge spiritual leverage.

Einstein said that you cannot solve a problem with the same mind that created it. The purpose of a problem is to motivate you to elevate your consciousness so you can see why it is a problem, and remedy it from higher ground. Without a spiritual perspective, we just slog along, bumping into obstacles, continually recreating the same problems, learning from trial and error (mostly error), and stretching our journey for endless agonizing epochs. Used wisely, spirituality is a time saver, trouble avoider, and pain reliever. It is the express route home.

Misapplied Metaphysics

The spiritual path can also become a distraction and delay our homecoming. We can misuse metaphysics as an excuse for not living responsibly, indulging the ego, and avoiding the lessons that can help us advance on our soul's journey. We can become so enamored with other-worldly phenomena that we miss the gifts and opportunities of this world. Some people are paranormal junkies, chasing spirits who will help them while they overlook people who love them; seeking gurus to tell them how to live while their own divine inner guidance is shouting at them from the inner rooftop; and trekking to remote power places while the power they seek lives within them. Others get "metaphysical indigestion," sampling so many different teachings that they grow muddled and master none. The mystic Ramakrishna likened spiritual seeking to a person digging many shallow wells and not finding water. To plumb the source of life, you need to dig deep. Any worthy path pursued with dedication and integrity will take you to the treasure. My teacher used to say, "Truth is like a diamond. If you follow any facet to the center, it will connect you to the nexus point of all the other facets."

Some people develop an identity as a spiritual seeker and do not go on to become a spiritual finder. They keep asking questions, but do not hear the answers they are given. Jesus said, "The kingdom of heaven is within you," and "The kingdom of heaven is at hand." These clues open the door to the presence of God right where you stand. The day you quit seeking and start finding is the turning point of a lifetime.

The Mystical Marriage

The Bible speaks of the "mystical marriage" which represents the harmonious integration of the spiritual and the physical, yin and yang, masculine and feminine, and the left and right sides of the brain. All of our life experiences help us bring this crucial marriage to the altar. It is a rare person who is naturally balanced. Most people are tilted toward one polarity or the other. Some are so immersed in the world that they are oblivious to the spiritual dimension, and they suffer because their lives feel empty and meaningless. Others are floating so far in the stratosphere that they miss the wisdom that earthly experiences deliver. A healthy life integrates both fields.

If you are out of balance, life will bring you the perfect situations to help you restore balance. You may lose your job because you are constantly late or make errors. Or you may get burnt out or ill from working too much. Or get a ticket because you forgot to renew your car's registration. Or get depressed after trying to save people who are not ready to be saved. The universe functions on homeostasis, constantly redirecting what is not of the Tao, the great flow of life, back to the Tao. Every challenge is a communication from the

Cosmic Center for Life Balance, saying, "Wake up! There is a gift here if you are willing to receive it!"

To succeed in life, you must find the meeting place of heaven and earth. *A Course in Miracles* tells us that the world is but a dream, and sadly a nightmare for many. Yet it is possible to have a happy dream in which the nature of the dream becomes joy, not sorrow. You will not create a happy dream by defining the three-dimensional world as the sole reality. You must incorporate a Higher Power, by whatever name you know It, into your worldly walk. Thus you consummate the marriage your soul has sought. While you may have long yearned for a life partner, what you are really seeking is the inner marriage of the apparently split parts of yourself. When you achieve that union, everything in the outside world, including a life partner, shows up naturally and effortlessly.

Master the Master Class

You took on a body and are in the world for a reason. The density of the physical plane and the contrast it generates offer unmistakable lessons that we might miss in a more etheric environment. The world is a master class for courageous souls willing to dive deep into illusion to discover the truth that illusion is hiding. You are a spiritual voyager, a soul investigating form through the passing experience of duality. Camp out here for a while, but don't attempt to build a permanent residence in a place where nothing is permanent. Our only real refuge is in spirit, which is impervious to the winds of outer change. There is a quiet place within you where the flame does not flicker.

The world is alluring but highly undependable; seductive but insecure. What most people consider normal is largely insane, not at all the way we were meant to live. You have become aware of a vaster truth that lifts you beyond the world and yields reward that nothing in form can deliver. The desire to escape the world is the healthiest desire you will ever have, for it calls you to rise beyond suffering rather than plunge deeper into it. But if you are going to escape the world, escape into truth, not another illusion. Align with a higher reality to bring the world into the light. If you have a job, family, and worldly responsibilities, use that playing field to develop mastery that will serve you and those you touch.

You were born to swim in the deep end of the pool, not drown in it. Make your worldly experience work on your behalf rather than getting lost in it. One way to find heaven is to leave the world. Another way is to lift the world closer to it.

DIRECT CONNECT 31
Feet on the Ground

Do you know people who are so immersed in spiritual phenomena that they make errors or cause problems because they are not grounded?

What kinds of missteps have you observed such people making?

How could they act in a more grounded fashion in order to achieve their tasks more effectively?

Do you ever make errors or missteps because you are not grounded? How so?

How could you be more effective by being more grounded?

What tools or techniques can you use to stay more grounded?

Do you know anyone who demonstrates a healthy balance between their spiritual life and their worldly activities? If so, who are they?

What can you learn from their role model and apply to make your life more effective?

✳ ✳ ✳

Affirm:

I walk with my head in the clouds and my feet on the ground.

*I am true to my spiritual path while
taking care of my worldly responsibilities.*

WHO YA GONNA CALL?

Students often ask Bashar if there are dark or demonic entities that can harm us. He explains that while such entities do exist in the world of illusion, they cannot harm or affect you if you are not a vibrational match to them. You may notice them, but they have no power over you if you are established in a higher, finer, lighter state of consciousness. If there is nothing in you equivalent to them, you are invisible to them, and they to you.

At the conclusion of an evening seminar, a woman approached me and asked if I would come to her house and "talk to the lady in the hall." She and her husband had just moved into their home, and apparently a ghost was haunting the place. I am not an exorcist, but I liked the challenge, so I went.

I did not see or feel any ghost, but just in case she was there, I commanded her to depart. I knew that no ghost has power in the presence of God, which I affirmed, and I said a prayer for release. After my self-styled exorcism, the couple thanked me and I went back to my hotel room and watched *Ghostbusters*.

Are ghosts, demons, and evil entities real? Can you be possessed? Can dark forces make you do bad things? Is there a devil that generates all the evil in the world? Daily the news shouts of countless twisted events driven by fear and illusion. Corruption infiltrates business, government, and religion, while deluded terrorists kill senselessly. It appears that the world has been hijacked by dark forces and we are vulnerable to all kinds of attacks.

Yet as a divine being created in the image and likeness of God, none of these people, events, or forces have any power over you. The Book of Timothy tells us, "For God has not given us a spirit of fear, but of power and of love and of a sound mind." When darkness and light meet, light prevails. When Jesus encountered a man possessed, he firmly commanded, "Satan, get out!" and the man was instantly released. No illusion can stand in the presence of God.

You, too, have the power to relieve suffering by calling forth the light in situations where darkness appears to rule. When eagles fly at a low altitude, crows sometimes peck at them. Yet the eagle's wingspan and strength are far greater than the crow's. The eagle simply ascends to an altitude the crows cannot reach. Likewise, negativity cannot touch you if you maintain a high consciousness. Illness and healing function at two distinctly different frequencies, like two radio stations playing radically different music or dialogue. When you fight evil as if it can harm you, you are stuck on the station it is occupying, and you fall prey to the falsities that drive it. Instead, reset your dial so you are established at a frequency that evil cannot reach. Jesus said, "Resist not evil, but overcome evil with good." Authentic teachers and healers are eagles who soar high, lift their students and patients on their broad wings, and teach them to fly on their own.

Marchers in the Night

I once camped out overnight with a friend at Maui's Iao Valley, one of the most mystical and enchanting places on the planet. Whenever I visit that sacred site, I feel deeply healed; it is truly a holy place. Late one afternoon before the park closed, we hiked deep into the valley and set up our tent before nightfall when visitors are required to exit. No other persons were anywhere in the park.

Just as we were getting ready to go to sleep, I heard the sound of a group of men chanting an ancient Hawaiian chant. I sat up and listened to hear it more clearly. I asked my friend, "Do you hear that?" He listened for a while and nodded. The chanting was unmistakable and powerful.

A few months later I visited the Pi'ilanihale Heiau, one of the largest remains of an ancient Hawaiian temple, in Hana, Maui. A friend who knew the heiau's caretakers took me to their home near the temple. They told me that they often see and hear spirits roaming the ruins at night. That jogged me to recount my Iao Valley encounter. The couple told me, "Those were the night marchers."

"Who are they?" I had to ask.

"The ghosts of ancient Hawaiian royalty and warriors, who roam remote areas at night. They replicate their historic processions from the mountains down to the ocean."

Goosebumps. (Or, as Hawaiians say, "chicken skin.")

The caretaker went to her bookshelf, pulled out a book, and opened it on a table before me. It was a graduate thesis that a University of Hawaii student had written about night marcher sightings. Many people, mostly fisherman, hunters, and campers, have not only heard but seen the ghostly processions. This is a well-documented and accepted phenomenon in those islands.

We accept people in physical bodies as real and we communicate with each other. The spirits that animate those bodies are just as alive, in some ways more real because they are the source of life in those bodies. Many people say they do not believe in invisible entities. Yet our world now depends almost entirely on invisible wireless signals we take for granted. People walk the streets of New York with small devices clipped to their ears and talk to people in Mumbai. Satellites beam countless packets of data to sustain the Internet and guide your car via GPS, detecting traffic jams ahead and alerting you to them. You see friends and relatives on FaceTime and groups of people on Zoom, no matter where they are on the planet. Just because someone is not physically present does not mean they are not spiritually present. The veil between the worlds is becoming thinner daily; the physical is not just yielding to the invisible, but relying on it. There is nothing spooky about spirits without bodies. In many ways, spirits *in* bodies are spookier, since many people have lost touch with their spiritual source and live distorted, painful lives. We are living at a time when the invisible is made visible, and the physical world we thought was so solid, is superseded and even managed by entities and energies our fingers cannot touch.

Which World Do You Live In?

A Course in Miracles tells us that there are really only two worlds: the world that God created, and the world the ego made up. God's world contains only the attributes of love: joy, kindness, compassion, forgiveness, creativity, inner peace, unity, life, and healing. The ego's world is the opposite in every way, characterized by separation, conflict, emptiness, defensiveness, suffering, and death. When we

are established in God's world, the world of fear is meaningless and has no power over our experience. When we are
absorbed in the ego's fabricated reality, the attributes of God
seem illusory, and we feel vulnerable at every turn. From the
viewpoint of God's world, the realm of fear is deluded and
powerless. The purpose of our human journey is to learn to
discern between the two worlds, choose love, and enjoy its
endless blessings.

Any form of evil is the offspring of ego, and is therefore
without substance and impotent. What gives evil *apparent*
reality is our belief in it, focusing on it, and acting on its dic-
tates. All power lives in the mind, so we must be extremely
careful where we point our mind, for in that choice we
determine the world we experience. In the *Star Trek* television episode "Wolf in the Fold," an invisible malevolent
entity invades the Starship Enterprise and takes possession
of its crew. One by one the crew members fall prey to the
invader's dark energy and engage in vicious acts, harming
each other and the vessel. Mayhem ensues until it appears
that the ship and its crew are doomed. Then the ship's com-
manders realize that the entity is feeding on fear. The more
the crew becomes afraid, the more they generate suffering;
and the more suffering they generate, the more afraid they
become. Dr. McCoy then concocts a tranquilizer that relaxes
the crew, soothes their emotions, and relieves them of fear.
The crew then becomes lighthearted and playful. With the
element of fear removed, the entity starves and departs,
returning the Enterprise and its crew to its natural state of
well-being.

The story is truer than fiction. The source of human sorrow and conflict is fear. When we quit feeding fear by acting
on it, all the effects of fear depart. If we could remove fear
as a motivator in human activity, the world would be an
entirely different place, like unto heaven. There would be no

wars, starvation would cease (most famines are the result of war), greed would unravel, and stress-related diseases (perhaps all of them) would disappear. While fear still runs the lives of the masses, each of us can choose to head in the direction of more love and less fear in our daily life. We can examine which of our actions are fear-based and which are love-based, asking ourselves, "What would I be doing differently if I were not afraid?" and then keep choosing in favor of the light.

The Match Game

Dark entities can influence, taunt, control, or possess only by agreement. To get hooked, you must be hookable. In such relationships there is a kind of Velcro interlocking in which the configuration of another person's or entity's hooks matches your configuration. Like attracts like. Withdraw your piece of the Velcro, or change the configuration of your hooks, and that's the end of the interaction. Fear and resistance are very tempting to hook with; they breed more of themselves. Love, inner peace, and connection to Higher Power reconfigure your hooks so that only higher-level entities can connect with you, and your interactions are healthy and rewarding.

When a student asked Hilda Charlton about the value of using a Ouija board, she replied, "Why consult a source that is just an inch above earth? There are higher and more benevolent entities available to contact." Like all human endeavors, occult sciences and practices have a light side and a dark side to them. They are valuable only if you align with the purer elements associated with them. If you get sucked into the darker elements, you are in for trouble.

The Indian sage Meher Baba talked about people trapped in a drinking habit. He said that discarnate spirits who were addicted to alcohol during their physical life hang around bars and get off on the feelings that drunk people emanate—a kind of vicarious alcoholism. These spiritual parasites exploit drinkers for their own gratification. For this reason, Meher Baba explained, liquor got the name "spirits" because drinkers attract spirits who take advantage of them. Such spirits might egg people on to keep drinking so the spirit can get more jollies from the human being's experience.

This is a good example of how people and entities interlock energy. People who drink heavily are a match to spirits who wish they could drink. The drunker people get, the more the spirits possess them. This is why people do stupid things when they drink, fall down and hurt themselves, get into fights, cause auto accidents, and commit crimes. They have given the power of their mind and body over to a dark stream of thought. Even if you don't believe in invisible spirits, it is obvious that people who get drunk are sucked into a vortex of negative thoughts, feelings, and intentions. They are participating in malevolent energy, and this negative agreement goes on to hurt themselves and others.

If you watch dark, scary, spooky, horror, war, or violent movies, you tap into the astral plane where negative energies rule. By focusing on them, you call them into your mind, heart, and home, and replicate that experience. (Groucho Marx described television as "a medium in which you invite into your living room people you would never let near your house.") I don't watch any movie that takes me to a reality I do not wish to dwell in. If you have trouble sleeping, have bad dreams, or wake up unrested and irritable, I suggest an experiment: Don't watch negative movies or the news before you go to bed. Don't do emails or work, discuss politics, or get into arguments with a family member. Instead, watch or read something uplifting, listen to enjoyable music, or immerse yourself in a relaxing, mind-quieting activity. If you practice this for just a short while you will sleep better, wake up refreshed, enjoy a significantly upgraded attitude, and your health will improve.

You can also use the dynamic of matching energies to interlock with positive spirits and keep them close to you. Angels, guides, and spiritual masters will aid you to live your best life and help others live theirs. You can attract benevolent entities through prayer, meditation, being in nature, listening to joyful music and uplifting teachings, engaging in meaningful conversations, and doing whatever puts you in an expanded state. When your spirits are high, you attract high spirits. Pray or affirm, *"I now open to connect with angels, guides, and masters dedicated to the light who will empower me to live at the highest level of divine expression."* Decorate your home or office with art and beauty, serving as windows to a higher dimension. Keep your area tidy, which raises the vibration. Choose relationships that empower you rather than drag you down. When you do your part to live in the light, Higher Power will do Its part and send you all the help you need, visible and invisible, to sustain your spiritual journey.

Just Because They're Dead Doesn't Mean They're Smart

Some people believe that if they can just connect with a departed relative or other nonphysical being, they will receive the guidance they need. This works if your relative or the entity is established in wisdom and love. But just as we must use discernment when communicating with human beings, we must exercise discernment when communicating with spiritual beings. Don't accept everything as true just because you believe it is coming from someone in another dimension. Try all guidance on for size to determine what matches you and what doesn't.

When people pass over, they do become "smarter" in that their field of vision and connection to Source extends far beyond the limits of perception prescribed by the world of the physical senses. Free from the blinders of the three-dimensional world, a soul gains broader multi-dimensional perspective. People without bodies can see beyond the earthly shadows and guide us from an expanded perspective.

Yet there are three factors that determine the quality of a message you receive from the spirit world: the source, the messenger, and the recipient. If the source is pure, the messenger is clear, and you as recipient are open, you will get a pure message that will help your life. If, however, any of those elements are distorted, confused, or sullied, you will get a garbled, less-than-helpful message. We have already looked at the factors that determine the quality of the source and the messenger. Now let's look into how your consciousness as the recipient affects your results.

The Law of Attraction provides that any entity you contact is a match to your own consciousness. If your mind and heart are open and you sincerely seek to grow spiritually, your psychic or channeled reading will take you there. If you are embroiled in drama, titillated by spooks, or doubtful of your worth, you will attract "guides" who reflect your state of mind. You are a casting director requesting a casting agency to provide an actor who fulfills the role you prescribe. Because you have free will and your mind is powerful, you can conjure any entity that matches the job description. If you are intent on hearing a particular answer, you may screen out all else and hear what you wish to hear rather than what is being said. If you have a strong desire to attain a particular material goal, you may not hear the spiritual wisdom the source is offering that supersedes the material goal. If you are in fear, you may interpret the message in a fearful way. If you are skeptical, you may dissect the reading to shreds and miss the gift being offered. What and how much you receive depends on your mindset.

This is why it is important to set your intention before asking for help. Prayer is your greatest ally. Before getting a reading or seeking guidance, ask Higher Power to send you information of the highest quality to create results in everyone's best interests. Such a sincere prayer will align you with healing and shield you from dark entities or garbled streams of consciousness. The best psychics say a prayer at the outset of their readings, asking that they be used in the most positive way and be most helpful to their client. Do the same for yourself, and you will set the stage for results that work.

Your Divine Protection

Because you are created in the image and likeness of God—literally a child of God—your heavenly Father/Mother has your back. Here is a simple affirmation you can use that will remind you of your divine protection, especially if you perceive any sense of danger:

> The power of God is within me.
>
> The grace of God surrounds me.

As a divine being, you have dominion over heaven and earth. You are unstoppable, unhurtable, and immortal. The strength of God is with you because you are an expression of God. You are loved and you are safe. When you know this, you manifest well-being in and around you. No evil being, human or spook, can disturb you. You are protected because you not only walk in light, but you *are* the light.

All evil and its manifestations are the offspring of erroneous thought, powerless in the face of divine love and light. The same mortal mind that gave illusions power can withdraw that power and reinvest it in truth and its manifestations. If you are faced with any dark energy, human or etheric, summon the power of God, which never fails because it is the only real power that exists. The One who spun galaxies into existence can take care of any problem the human mind perceives. All other seeming powers dissolve in the presence of pure love. Know and practice this master truth, and you are free.

DIRECT CONNECT 32
Angels and Demons

Do you believe there are demonic entities who can trouble or possess you or others?

Have you ever had an encounter with an entity from the dark side?

If so, how did you respond?

How do you think that dark forces, if they exist, accomplish their goals?

Do you have faith that there is a Power greater than evil? Are you protected?

What do you think is good way to deal with the appearance of a negative force, should you encounter it?

How do you think Jesus Christ and other healers dispersed dark forces?

What prayer or affirmation might you say in the face of the appearance of a dark force?

THE GREAT HOMECOMING

Our spiritual journey culminates in the recognition that all apparently external guides are really the One God, our True Self, reaching us in ways we can accept and understand. While physical and nonphysical teachers appear to teach us, it is the Teacher who educates. If we are not ready to relate to the One directly, in compassion the One sends teachers to meet us where we stand, and usher us to the next level. Like the initial booster stages of a rocket fall away after the craft has escaped the earth's atmosphere, external teachers fall away as we stretch to explore the farther reaches of inner space.

Ultimately everything and everyone in form resolves into light. Angels and demons, spirits and bodies, channelers and entities, teachers and students, truth and deception, good and evil, compassion and cruelty, life and death, are all illusions through which we pass. Anything that has an opposite, or ends, is not the whole truth. Reality, meanwhile, is unshakeable. When we awaken from the dreams of suffering and death, we realize that our real self has never been touched, marred, or changed in any way. We are as whole and innocent as the day we were created. Our departure from home was in thought only; in truth, we never left.

FRIENDS IN HIGH PLACES

There is no place like home because there is no place *but* home. All journeys lead us to our divine nature, which we carried with us all along, simply awaiting our recognition.

Stage 5 of Spiritual Evolution

We now go beyond all external guidance and we connect directly with the God within us. We no longer require an intermediary to reveal reality. The life-changing insights that the great masters, physical and nonphysical, have imparted, are available to us directly. We grow beyond a belief in spiritual hierarchies, and we claim our identity as an expression of God. We come home to our original self as a divine being. The truth we seemed to be importing from outside lived within us all the while, and we celebrate the Great Homecoming.

Like the prodigal son who renounced his legacy, became lost in a far country, and yearned to inherit his true estate, our heavenly Father has faith in us even while we wallow in illusions. He forgives our errors, shines light on our path, and welcomes us with open arms. Love cares for us even when we thought it was absent. Whether or not we will arrive home is not the question—that is assured. When and how we arrive is up to us.

Blessed are all the teachers and teachings, physical and nonphysical, we encounter along the way. They are messengers of God. Blessed are you as you serve as a messenger to help others find their way. We seek to know angels because we seek to know the angel we are. All of the masters you have ever met live within you, as you. All journeys lead to the recognition that you are what you seek, you are eternally whole, and you are innocent and perfect to the core of your being. In the end, there is only love.

ACKNOWLEDGMENTS

In a book illuminating great teachers and teachings, first gratitude must go to the masters I have been blessed to learn from, physical and nonphysical. I bow to the grace of God as the source of my relationship with all the entities and channelers I describe. My awakening and healing as a result of their teaching goes beyond what words can capture. My deepest thanks to all of my teachers, mentors, and healers. I am richly blessed, as we all are.

My ongoing deep gratitude to my beloved partner Dee, who supports me personally and professionally, and offers her gracious love and insight to enhance the quality of this work.

I so appreciate Debby Handrich and medium Liz Winter, who kindly took the time and caring to read the book and give me their valuable opinions and suggestions.

My longtime friend Deborah Gordan served as a valuable resource to be sure that my recount of her mother Carla Gordan's teachings are clear and accurate.

The quality of the presentation has been magnificently enhanced by Natascha Bohmann, whose proofreading and editing have helped bring the book into its clearest presentation.

Once again I so appreciate the talented and so very helpful Riann Bender for her brilliant interior book design.

Graphic designer Elena Karampouli is a gift from the universe. Her book covers continue to amaze and inspire me.

Thank you, reader, for your courage to walk the spiritual journey, and add to the light of the world. We are all in this together.

ABOUT THE AUTHOR

Alan Cohen, M.A., holds degrees in psychology and human organizational development. He is the author of thirty popular inspirational books, including the best-selling *A Course in Miracles Made Easy* and the award-winning *A Deep Breath of Life*. He is a contributing writer for the #1 *New York Times* best-selling series *Chicken Soup for the Soul*, and he is featured in the book *101 Top Experts Who Help Us Improve Our Lives*. His books have been translated into 32 foreign languages. Alan has taught at Montclair State College, Omega Institute for Holistic Studies, and en*theos Academy for Optimal Living. He is a featured presenter in the award-winning documentary *Finding Joe*, celebrating the teachings of Joseph Campbell. His work has been presented on CNN and Oprah.com and in *USA Today, The Washington Post*, and *Huffington Post*. His monthly column *From the Heart* is published in magazines internationally. Alan is the founder and Director of the Foundation for Holistic Life Coaching. He presents programs on themes of life mastery, spiritual development, and positive self-image psychology. For information on Alan Cohen's books, seminars, holistic life coach training, videos, and audio recordings, visit:

www.alancohen.com

Learn More
with Alan Cohen

If you have enjoyed and benefited from *Friends in High Places,* you may want to deepen your understanding and inspiration by participating in Alan Cohen's in-person seminars, online courses, life coach training, or online subscription programs.

Inspirational Quote for the Day—An uplifting idea e-mailed to you each day (free)

Monthly e-Newsletter—Insightful articles and announcements of upcoming events (free)

A Weekly Wave of Sanity—YouTube live presentation of inspiring ideas

Live Webinars—Interactive uplifting programs on topics relevant to spirituality, self-empowerment, and holistic living

Online Courses—In-depth experiential exploration of *Friends in High Places,* healing, relationships, prosperity, prayer, metaphysics, and stress management

Life Coach Training—Become a certified professional holistic life coach or enhance your career and personal life with coaching skills

***A Course in Miracles* Retreat**—A residential program to empower you to master the principles and skills of this life-changing course

For information on these and other programs,
books, and recordings, visit

www.alancohen.com

Made in the USA
Columbia, SC
12 November 2021

48817678R00143